D1253491

AFRICAN CHRISTIAN THEOLOGY— ADAPTATION OR INCARNATION?

African Christian Theology — Adaptation or Incarnation?

Aylward Shorter

ORBIS BOOKS

Maryknoll, New York 10545

1977

The U.S. edition has been printed in photo offset from the original British edition by special arrangement with Geoffrey Chapman Publishers

Copyright © 1975 Geoffrey Chapman Publishers, London

Manufactured in the United States of America

Library of Congress Cataloging in Publication Data

Shorter, Aylward
    African Christian theology.

    Includes bibliographical references and index.
    1. Africa—Religion. 2. Christianity—Africa.
3. Theology, Doctrinal—History—Africa. I. Title.
BL2400.S42 1977   230'.096   77-23325
ISBN 0-88344-002-4
ISBN 0-88344-003-2 pbk.

FOR MY NEPHEWS AND NIECES
JACQUELINE, GEORGINA,
WILLIAM, EDWARD, GILES, DAMIAN, CECILIA,
TRISTRAM, HUGO, AND ORLANDO

Contents

viii

Introduction

The broad aim of this book is to show how African Christian Theology must grow out of a dialogue between Christianity and the theologies of African Traditional Religion. A further aim is to examine the various ways of studying and understanding African Traditional Religion, with a view to discovering the most effective methods. In speaking of Christianity, I do not want to limit myself to any particular church tradition, although as a Roman Catholic, it is perhaps natural that I should give evidence of greater familiarity with Roman Catholicism and its attitudes to the topic in hand. It will become clearer what is meant by African Traditional Religion as the discussion unfolds, but it would be advisable to try to say something about it right from the start. In using this term, I want to refer to the religious values, beliefs and practices which derive from the religious systems of non-Christian Africa. These religious systems were identified with the various ethnic cultures of pre-colonial Africa, and flourished before the coming of the western missionary and the western administrator. Although they were separate and self-contained systems, they interacted with one another and influenced one another to different degrees. This justifies our using the term African Traditional Religion in the singular to refer to the whole African religious phenomenon, even if we are, in fact, dealing with a multiplicity of theologies. Because of the link with the past, we are justified in using the term 'Traditional', but it must be borne in mind that we are dealing with a living tradition, and that this tradition has undergone drastic changes during and after the colonial era. Many, if not most, of the visible aspects—rites, practices and institutions—have disappeared, or are disappearing rapidly. However, this is not to say that African Traditional Religion is disappearing. On the contrary, traditional values and outlooks continue to live on and to exercise an influence among all sections of the population, including *bona fide* Christians and Muslims. Furthermore, these values have often found new life in neo-traditional religious movements and in the Independent African Churches. In speaking, therefore, of African Traditional Religion, we are speaking of a complex, developing phenomenon, and one which, though visibly changing, is far from moribund.

The term 'Christian' should be clear enough. I occasionally resort to the word 'Post-Christian' to describe people who have explicitly or effectively repudiated their Christian profession. Often these come from academic circles. The practitioner of African Traditional Religion, or the one who subscribes to the values, beliefs and outlooks of African Traditional Religion, is referred to in these pages by the rather clumsy phrase: 'African Traditional Religionist'. I have tried at all times to eschew the opprobrious term 'Pagan' and, as far as possible (not always possible!) the negative term: 'Non-Christian'. I willingly grant that very often the professing Christian is a crypto-African-Traditional-Religionist, and so the term is not meant necessarily to exclude Christians.

We begin by discussing the main channels and the main obstacles in conducting dialogue with African Traditional Religion. This leads us to consider the two other options, besides that of a synthesis deriving from dialogue. These are: syncretism and what I have called 'taking sides'. Syncretism, I take to be the juxtaposition of elements that are not integrated, and it is therefore, for me, a pejorative term. 'Taking sides' means consciously emphasizing either Christianity or African Traditional Religion to the exclusion of the other. Having opted for dialogue, we must then consider the current expectations for an African Theology and examine the need for a dialogical theology in Africa. This confronts us with the central problem of the book: How do we make a comparative study of the extremely complex phenomenon of African Traditional Religion? An examination of all the methods used or proposed becomes necessary, and we must adopt some and reject others.

In the chapters that follow, we shall offer some examples of the favoured methods, hinting, at the same time, at possible interchange between Christian and African Traditional Themes and Values. The study of African Traditional Religion must be systematic, making use of the human sciences, of history and of the scientific study of religion. However, science itself is a product of culture, and the question whether there can be real communication between cultures has to be faced. The answer that emerges from the consideration of this question paves the way for the theological universalism which is the object of an African Dialogical Theology. A study of the processes of pluralism and change in the modern world confirms that it is this kind of theological universalism that we must aim for.

Adaptation or Incarnation? This was the question asked by the Bishops of Africa and Madagascar at the 1974 Roman Synod. It was a controversial question and one fraught with possible misunderstandings. In opting for an incarnational theology we must safeguard both authenticity and catholicity. The debate is one example of a growing realization among Christians of the need for dialogue with the religious cultures of the Non-Christian world, and we shall consider the recent call for a ministry of dialogue in English-speaking Africa. Finally, we shall consider some practical conclusions for the religious educator of African youth, the generation that stands at the very heart of the conflict between two traditions.

Little of this present work has appeared before in published form. The first chapter is based on a paper presented to the Consultation organized at Gaba Pastoral Institute by the Vatican Secretariat for Non-Christian Religions, on Dialogue with African Traditional Religion. This meeting was held in August 1974. The second chapter is an amplification of an essay which appeared in Gaba Pastoral Paper No. 22, *The African Contribution to World Church and Other Essays*, Gaba, (Offset) 1972. Chapter Three is, again, a much more extended version of a scheme that appeared in *Prayer in the Religious Traditions of Africa*, Oxford University Press, Nairobi, 1974. Here the attempt has been made, not merely to list the different methods of study, but to work them out in full and to give examples. Chapter Four is based on a paper presented to the Third Conference on the Historical Study of African Religion, held at Limuru, Kenya, in

June 1974. In its present form, it has benefited by the discussion which took place at the conference with historians and Africanists from all over the world. In its original form, Chapter Five was a lecture given to Social Anthropology students at Makerere University in 1970 and 1971. Chapter Six is a development of ideas selected from the book mentioned in connection with Chapter Three, while Chapter Seven is largely new material. Chapter Eight is new material, except for section 5 which is based on a lecture given to the Roman Catholic Bishops of Uganda in November 1974. Finally, Chapter Nine is also new, with the exception of section 3 which is based on part of an article that appeared in the *African Ecclesiastical Review*, No. 4 of 1972, pp. 304-317. I wish to acknowledge the help given to me in developing these ideas by the various audiences in Africa to whom, in one form or another, different sections of this material were presented.

Aylward Shorter,
Gaba Pastoral Institute,
Kampala.

Chapter I

Meeting African Traditional Religion

1 The Demands of Dialogue

The basic demand of dialogue is duality. No dialogue is possible unless there are two sides or two persons ready to engage in it. When it begins, it takes the form of an exchange between two sides, a mutual address and response. This exchange is, moreover, a serious exchange, a confrontation of beings, a meeting of meanings, values, attitudes and understandings. To maintain the flow of meaning between the two sides other demands have to be met, and these largely take the form of barriers to be overcome. Such barriers are prejudice, differences of language and imagery, contrary purposes, anxiety and defensiveness. Dialogue is impeded if one side sees the other as a threat. Instead there is need for courage and humility—courage to take risks and humility to accept the possibility of undergoing a change oneself. This mutual awareness that constitutes dialogue is the essential ingredient of fellowship and love. It is also a precondition for true conversion of heart.[1]

In the light of these remarks about dialogue, the most basic question that can be asked about the Christian Church's dialogue with African Traditional Religion is: Are there really two sides? Is there really an exchange between two religions? African Traditional Religion has always been, to some extent, a submerged religion, indistinguishable from a cultural tradition. On the other hand, Christianity professes to be identifiable with each and every human culture. Its claim is that it is Catholic or universal. African Traditional Religion was tolerant and absorbent of new religious elements, not experiencing any necessity to misrepresent or proselytize other religions or their adherents. Christianity, on the other hand, is conscious of offering a challenge, and in the era of its first contacts with Africa it tended to be

5

uncompromising and intolerant—even violent. The paradox is an interesting one. Christianity cannot afford to stand outside a culture as something foreign or alien, even when that culture is ultimately identified with another religion; while, on the other hand, African Traditional Religion is unable to reject or withstand the influence of another religion even if that religion appears intolerant and hostile.

Dialogue is possible in so far as Christianity, seeking to penetrate African culture, is conscious of the religious tradition that underlies it. It is also possible in so far as African Traditional Religion, in its uncritical eagerness to appropriate foreign elements, becomes conscious of Christianity as a distinct religious system. If this does not happen, the religions will not meet and there will be a double monologue rather than a dialogue. Syncretism is the absence of dialogue or, perhaps, the failure of dialogue; to avoid it, there must be a continuous and consistent exchange of meanings. There is no use in the Church adapting to a false or incomplete picture of African culture. Nor is there any breakthrough when a Muganda diviner in Kampala employs the Apostle Matthew as a spirit-familiar, or when the Blessed Virgin Mary becomes one of the hero-spirits in a Chwezi possession cult.[2] Unless it is to forfeit its claim to Catholicity, Christianity cannot afford to reject the dialogue with African Traditional Religion. Unless it is to be faced with irrelevance or even extinction as a visible tradition, African Traditional Religion cannot afford to reject the dialogue with Christianity. The rest of this chapter, therefore, and, indeed, the rest of this book will be devoted to the question of how the barriers to dialogue can be overcome, and of how a real confrontation and meeting can take place.

The Concept of Non-Verbal Dialogue

We have noted that differences of language and imagery may constitute a barrier to dialogue. The first stage is obviously to set about learning the other person's language and to study the signs and symbols he uses. A much more radical barrier exists when one side assumes that the communication will be verbal, while the other side is incapable of adequate verbal communication. This is, in fact, the case with the dialogue between Christianity and African Traditional Religion. Christianity is a 'Religion of the Book', a

6

highly literate religion with a long tradition of theological exposition, written and oral. Ritual has played no mean part in Christian life and worship, but the chosen means of communication has always been pre-eminently verbal. African Traditional Religion, on the other hand, is not only historically pre-literate, it is by choice not even always orally articulate. It has been said with some truth that 'the African dances out his ideas', and certainly the dramatic and ritual expression of ideas through symbolic action is more important to African Traditional Religion than verbalization. What is more, even in its oral 'texts' of poetry, song, invocations and ritual formulas, African Traditional Religion employs a symbolism and imagery that cannot easily be translated into purely rational, verbalized concepts without doing violence to their meaning. Symbolism appeals to experience and cannot be understood except through a sharing of the experience to which it refers. The African Traditional Religionist is not often capable of giving an exegetical explanation of a symbol or ritual. On the contrary, he is much more likely to explain one symbol by referring to another symbol, and the enquirer finds himself in an even more complex and confusing situation than before. The meaning of a symbol or ritual can usually only be deduced from the observed operation of the symbolic elements in their immediate context, or from their observed position in the whole structure of symbolism proper to the culture.[3]

It follows that the African Traditional Religionist can only be a successful spokesman for his own tradition if he acquires these techniques of observation and analysis. Either that, or the Christian must, himself, acquire these techniques of participant observation in order to encounter the authentic meanings of African Traditional Religion expressed in their original forms. The first alternative would certainly lead to the possibility of a dialogue in verbal terms, using the communications conventions of literate cultures. Being himself literate and highly educated, the African Traditional Religionist would not only be able to verbalize his own tradition, he would also understand—presumably—the written traditions of Christianity and encounter authentic Christian meanings. It is a happy, blissful picture, that of this exponent of African Traditional Religion holding forth among the scribes and the doctors of the Christian Schools. Alas, it is not drawn from life. The pressures of modern education and the demands of the school and university environment ensure that the African abandons his commitment to Traditional Religion long before he can acquire the techniques necessary for a sophisticated understanding of it. Whatever nostalgia or sympathy he may feel for African Traditional Religion, the African student of the subject is invariably either a Christian or a Post-Christian, a professing adherent of a Church, or a non-denominational believer or agnostic. Even if he is a Post-Christian, he comes to the study of his subject as much an outsider as the Christian himself.

The second alternative is, therefore, the more realistic one. Dialogue with African Traditional Religion, although it can afterwards be written up by the Christian party, must be essentially non-verbal. It can only really take place through mutual participation in experience. The Christian should take the initiative, seeking to experience through participant observation, not only African Traditional Religion, but also the reactions of the African Traditional Religionist to the experience of Christianity. The important stages are threefold: experience of African Traditional Religion by a Christian as a Christian; experience of Christianity by an African Traditional Religionist as an African Traditional Religionist; the systematic interpretation and reporting of these experiences. In the writing published to date, there has been considerable concern shown by Christians to understand and interpret African Traditional Religion, although far too little of this work is based on first-hand experience. Virtually no concern whatever has been shown for the understanding of Christianity by African Traditional Religion. This is largely because the non-verbal character of the dialogue has been neglected, and when this is neglected, dialogue—in this case—disappears.

3 Dialogue Versus Closed Systems of Thought

The concept of the closed society was popularized by Karl R. Popper.[4] In contrast to the open society, the closed society is characterized by an unselfconsciousness that accounts for a complete absence of rational planning. Although it is subject to regular internal renewal and change, there is no possibility of it undergoing a change of structure or organization. No criticism is tolerated in the closed society and there are no alternative courses of action to which its members can appeal. It is ignorant of everything save its own socio-cultural inheritance. Of course, not even Popper believed that a society could be completely and hermetically closed. If they were completely closed there would be no possibility of open societies ever developing. The historical dimension is crucial, and this dimension includes external interaction and contact. The closed character of some societies is therefore a matter of degree, and as such is a useful concept when speaking about barriers to dialogue. It is obvious that persons whose thinking is closed cannot engage in dialogue. There has to be openness of thought on either side and a readiness to accept alternatives as, at least, a possibility.

The ethnically based cultures and thought-systems of traditional Africa were typically closed in Popper's sense. There was little possibility of change occurring from within the social organism, apart from the regular renewal of the organism itself and the development and improvement of its symbolic structure. Face to face with this type of thought-system came the Church of nineteenth-century Europe, a Church which, for its part also, had many of the characteristics of the closed system. The tragedy is that early missionary endeavour in Africa never produced a confrontation or a meeting of meanings between African religious thought-systems and the thinking of nineteenth-century European Christianity. They represented two outlooks which, if they were not entirely exclusive, nevertheless remained mutually closed to one another. Even when the ethnographic researches of Christian missionaries revealed the new riches of African religious thought to the world, an undeveloped theology of salvation prevented any exchange from taking place, and the Church was resigned to condemning the very object of her interest and study.

Fortunately, the discovery of the non-Christian religions brought about in its turn a development of salvation theology. Non-Christian religions were no longer looked upon by Christians with a truculent sense of superiority, if not of downright hostility. In the words of the Second Vatican Council, 'The Catholic Church ... looks with sincere respect upon those ways of conduct and of life, those rules and teachings which, though differing in many particulars from what she holds and sets forth, nevertheless reflect a ray of that Truth which enlightens all men.'[5] From the side of the Church at least, dialogue with the African Religions is now a possibility. What has happened on the side of African Traditional Religion? It was not to be expected that African Traditional Religion would be affected by theological developments within Christianity—at least until these developments made themselves pastorally felt. African Traditional Religion, however, was not completely unaffected by the proximity of missionary Christianity. Even if Christianity took no cognizance of African insights, African religious ideas were sometimes reinforced or clarified, as Monica Wilson has shown for the Nyakyusa of Tanzania.[6] This, however, was hardly a conscious process and one cannot talk about an exchange taking place when one side rejected and despised the other.

During the past hundred years African Traditional Religion has been visibly sinking beneath the surface of modern social life in Africa, but what remains above the surface is, in fact, the tip of an iceberg. At Baptism, the African Christian repudiates remarkably little of his former non-Christian outlook. He may be obliged to turn his back upon certain traditional practices which the Church, rightly or wrongly, has condemned in his area, but he is not asked to recant a religious philosophy. The Church, in any case, takes no cognizance of this philosophy. Consequently, he returns to the forbidden practices as occasion arises with remarkable ease. Conversion to Christianity is for him sheer gain, an 'extra' for which he has opted. It is an overlay on his original, religious culture. Apart from the superficial condemnations, Christianity has really had little to say about African Traditional Religion in the way of serious judgements of value. Consequently, the African Christian operates with two thought-systems at once, and both of them are closed to each other. Each is only superficially modified by the other. It becomes clear, therefore, that the heart of the dialogue between Christianity and African Traditional Religion is located within the consciousness of the African Christian himself. It is there that the most serious exchange must take place. When the African Christian who has experienced this dialogue within himself possesses the necessary techniques of interpretation and exposition alluded to above, then the dialogue will become verbally explicit.

In 1969 a Catholic scholar-bishop, Mgr James Komba of Songea, Tanzania, mounted the platform at a conference on African Religion at the University of Dar-es-Salaam, and spoke in simple and moving terms of the debate and conflict between two religious philosophies that had taken place within him as a young man. There was not an academic present who did not feel it a privilege to listen to him. This is the very stuff of Christian-African dialogue. Basically, it is the same process at work in the writings of African Christian scholars like Professor J. S. Mbiti, Professor E. B. Idowu, Canon H. Sawyerr, and Fr Charles Nyamiti. This is no criticism of their work, on the contrary, as we have already observed, rigorous scientific standards are as much in demand for dialogue as for any branch of learning. What has to be accepted is that it is generally impossible to approach the study of African Traditional Religion without at least an implicit dialogue with the Christianity or Post-Christianity of the scholar carrying out the study. The African Christian, therefore, must come to judge each of the closed outlooks in terms of the other. He must come to accept or to reject them, to integrate them or to take sides with one or other. Taking sides, as we shall see in the following section, is another possibility. At all events there has to be an opening and dialogue must defeat the closed thought-system.

4 Dialogue with a Living Tradition

A temptation that has to be avoided (but which seldom is!) in the study of African Traditional Religion is that of being an antiquarian. It is easy to fall into the trap of studying a religion of the past, the religion of the traditional African whose religion-centred career is traced in minute detail from the cradle to the grave. Quite a number of popular works are concerned with the life-cycle of this traditional African. The assumption is that African Religion must be described in its pure and pristine form, before it became adulterated and decayed as a result of contact with foreign cultures and of modernization. Obviously, the historical study of African religion is a fundamental necessity if we are to understand contemporary developments, but it must be a genuine historical exercise, appealing to genuine, historical evidence. It is not enough to paint a hypothetical, glowing picture of religion in the everyday life of Africans in the past. Still

11

less should one assume that Christians must enter into dialogue with a dead or dying tradition. The 'traditional African' who is proverbially so religious no longer exists, and his ghost must be laid. Our dialogue is to take place with a living tradition, a dynamic religion in which there are new areas of application as well as continuities with the past.

African Traditional Religion was never wholly particularist, and historical research is revealing ever more clearly that religious concepts, symbols and practices had a currency wider than other elements of an ethnically based culture. Religious movements, cults and objects were subject to historical diffusion. On the other hand, African Traditional Religion did have an ethnic basis in the sense that it was wholly articulated through the socio-political institutions of the tribe. However much religious concepts and symbols transcended the horizons of tribal culture, the African could only experience his religion and give expression to it through the structures of the tribe.

Multiple adaptations, in relative isolation, to differing environments, and affecting very small populations, had produced the fragmented, autonomous groupings that we commonly call 'tribes', and it was in the tribe that African Traditional Religion received its visible expression. Authority in traditional Africa was basically politico-religious and professional priesthoods and other cultic offices or forms of religious dedication represented partial approaches or specializations within the religious system taken as a whole. At the universal or territorial level it was the hierarchy of family-heads, clan-leaders, elders and chiefs who presided over religious rituals, led the people in worship and took the initiative in creating and manipulating religious institutions such as oracles or rites of initiation.

Tribal loyalty has certainly not lost its importance today, as we enter the last quarter of the twentieth century. Some would argue that it is stronger and more resilient than ever before. However, it cannot be denied that the tribe has undergone a radical transformation. From being a more or less autonomous political unit, with its own socio-political institutions and autonomy, it has now developed into an ideology of unity or a symbol of cultural identity. The ancient communitarian rituals and territorial cults have been weakened beyond recall, if they have not completely disappeared, and religious activity today operates on an individual or a family basis only. In so far as the religious specialists continue to meet an individual or a family need, they survive in an attenuated fashion, but the other visible expressions of the traditional religion have succumbed along with the tribal authorities responsible for them. In spite of this, dialogue with such practitioners as survive may still be well worthwhile.

It has already been suggested that the religious traditions of Africa are going underground and that they are managing to co-exist as closed systems with the missionary religions. While this remains true, it is also a fact that certain, new, visible forms of African Traditional Religion are coming into existence in the shape of what Victor Turner has called 'communities of affliction'.[7] These are voluntary associations, more or less religious in character, which cater for sick people and people in need of status definition. In many, if not most, cases they include a form of spirit mediumship and a greater or lesser importance is attached to glossolalia. Mary Douglas has made the interesting suggestion that such movements are a symbolic commentary on the sickness of the old social order,[8] but even if they are a temporary phenomenon in the religious development of Africa, it would repay the Church to undertake dialogue with them in view of the revival of Pentecostalism within Christianity and of the problem of pastoral care for the sick in Africa. Many of these movements are crudely syncretistic, incorporating elements from Christianity and from western culture. In many cases, too, the Church's attitude to them is naïvely hostile and anachronistic, applying to them outmoded stereotypes of diabolical possession, devil worship and so forth.[9]

African religious traditions also find a new lease of life in some of the African Independent Churches. These are by no means a homogeneous group—quite the contrary. Following the suggestions of Harold Turner,[10] we may identify three main categories: the Christian, the Hebraist and the Neo-Traditional. In the Christian type, the differences with the parent mission Churches are historical rather than theological. In the Hebraist type is found a form of neo-Judaism with varying emphases on aspects of the Old Testament tradition. In the Neo-Traditional type there is a conscious revival or development of African Traditional

Religion. All these types of Church may possess an element of syncretism in which either a Judeo-Christian tradition meets an African Religious Tradition on Judeo-Christian terms, or an African Tradition meets Judaism and Christianity on African Traditional terms. It is, however, in the Neo-Traditional type of Independent Church that a dialogue would, perhaps, be most fruitful, seeing that it is in this type of Church that the African Tradition is most fully expressed.

Finally, there is the undisclosed presence of African Traditional Religion within the Historic Churches and Islam. In the case of Islam, the 'closed-system' model may not be entirely relevant. Indeed, some authors would argue that its relationship with African Traditional Religion has been marked by such openness that Traditional Religion has largely succeeded in absorbing it on its own terms.[11] In spite of this, however, there are different levels and degrees of absorption, corresponding to the different social classes and styles of life. It is interesting to speculate whether anything like this has happened to Christianity. Apart from the closed-system situation which is evidently widely applicable, it has been suggested that in some areas the basic tenets and moral injunctions of African Traditional Religion continue to thrive within official Christianity, unaffected by the addition of a few novelties (chiefly in the sphere of worship) which are typically Christian, and that a quiet absorption of Christianity has taken place which is all the more disturbing for its unconsciousness and insidiousness. Tanner came to this kind of conclusion after studying the extempore prayers of Tanzanian adolescents at Christian schools.[12] He found, for example, that the majority of prayers addressed God in largely traditional terms without reference to Christ or the Holy Spirit. Moreover, the vast majority took the form of unqualified petition with no elements of praise, adoration or thanksgiving. Deniel in Upper Volta concluded his study with the following words: 'We are obliged to conclude that at the level of morals and morality there is no essential difference between Islam, Christianity and Animism.'[13] While Philip Turner, in Uganda, believes that Christianity has 'over-adapted' to traditional authoritarianism and to the politico-religious structures of a closed African system,[14] If there is truth in such conclusions, then we are faced with a syncretism that is, perhaps, more serious than the failure of closed systems to confront one another.

At the academic level there is a parallel danger of taking a minimalist approach to Christianity. The Church's new positive attitude to African Traditional Religion may have an effect like that of a strong dose of alcohol on a weak head. The heady wine of nationalism and African self-affirmation may also tempt the African scholar and Christian and give him ultimately an altogether too roseate picture of African Traditional Religion. He may be tempted to emphasize only those areas of Traditional Religion which obviously overlap with Christianity, or, seeing that all academic study of African Religions is in some sense a dialogue, he may unconsciously attribute Christian values and meanings to the religions he is studying. To produce and to advocate such a synthesis is no bad thing; it is even a service to Christianity in Africa. The danger consists, as always, in the lack of self-awareness, and in what we referred to earlier as the taking of sides. Being (wrongly) convinced that African Traditional Religion and Christianity are identical, or at least interchangeable, the African scholar naturally opts for the African system, thus failing to give credit where it is due—to the challenge offered by Christianity. In the final analysis, a dialogue that has no self-awareness is just another form of syncretism. The Church must put its own house in order, recognizing the latent syncretism in its own life, thought and practice. This it can only do by engaging in valid and conscious dialogue.

5 *The Conscious Aims of Dialogue*

In spite of talk about Ecumenism and collaboration for the sake of national unity, the religions and religious systems of Africa are largely self-isolated and incapsulated. To their own way of thinking, they are still very much in competition with one another. At worst there is a completely closed situation; at best, a certain degree of syncretism. It can hardly be said that there is dialogue. Yet, in spite of their failure to communicate, the religious systems may each be fulfilling a particular need or emphasis in the life of the community. This social phenomenon is what Professor Murphree has called 'dialectical interchange'.[15] Religion does not, he argues, divide the Shona (Rhodesia) community. On the contrary, each form of religion caters for needs not catered for by others. Roman Catholics serve the community through education, in the running of schools. They also satisfy a craving for ritual and have exerted some influence in this regard on the local Independent Church, the Vapostori. Although Roman Catholics share certain cognate values and qualities with practitioners of the African Traditional Religion, the freer organization of the Methodists permits more initiative in adaptation than the legalistic tendencies of the Roman Catholics. Traditional Religion, as usual, pervades and permeates the whole fabric of Shona society but a specific interest in spirit possession, exorcism and witch-finding unites it with the Independent Church.

To discover this dialectic between the religious systems is a fascinating exercise, but, as we have insisted above, it remains a form of syncretism as long as it fails to gain consciousness. Dialogue begins when the religions first become aware of what they owe to each other. Thereafter real interaction and growth are possible. If dialogue could be established within and between the various forms of Christianity in Africa, the vestiges of visible African Traditional Religion, the Independent Churches and such movements as the communities of affliction, then such an outcome could be expected. The partners in the dialogue could learn from each other's strengths and weaknesses, from each other's successes and failures. Such dialogue, as we pointed out at the beginning of this chapter, requires humility, the acceptance of risk and the prospect of change.

What, in actual fact, would be the fruit of such dialogue between the Church and African Traditional Religion? First of all, there is the highly probable discovery of a large area of agreement between the two outlooks. The Church is already very favourably disposed to look for such agreement, and ideas such as 'preparation for the Gospel' and 'seeds of the Gospel' are already familiar from the texts of the Vatican Council. However, one cannot and one must not be satisfied with a search for parallels and concordances. This is to be guilty of saying to one's partner: 'How like you are to me! We can be friends because you resemble me!' Dialogue must be realistic. If there is the probability of a large area of agreement, there is an equal probability of a large measure of disagreement, even of fundamental difference of outlook. It may be possible to resolve some of the differences, but some will necessarily remain, and the Christian, even if he cannot make such attitudes his own, must try to understand them. Thirdly, there is the possibility of a divergence of interests. In this case it is not simply a question of different solutions being offered to fundamental human problems, it has to be recognized that different questions are being asked and different assumptions being made. As Professor Zaehner has written, any similarity that exists between the various religions of the world 'proves not that there is an inner unity underlying' them, but, he adds hopefully, 'that there is in man a craving for an incarnate God strong enough to force its way into the most uncompromising religious systems'.[16] If this is true, then existing divergence does not necessarily imply that convergence is impossible. Once more, we have a strong reason for engaging in dialogue.

Finally, there is the possibility of genuine interaction, bringing about changes in both partners to the dialogue. Interaction can mean a mutual, beneficial influence, whereby one outlook stimulates the development of the other. It can bring to light a hidden potential in each tradition in the form of latent themes or in the growth and reformulation of doctrine. Pledged, as the Church in Africa is, to the establishment of an 'African Christianity', such prospects should be welcome. The phrases 'preparation for the Gospel' and 'seeds of the Gospel' should not be interpreted to mean that Christianity is closed and static or that the religious experience of Traditional Africa is merely a preparation for the Church that we ourselves know. Dialogue between Christianity and African Traditional Religion is without doubt part of God's plan. If it were not, the missionary expansion of Christianity within Africa would not have taken place. As we have shown, the very presence of the Church in Africa demands dialogue for its own health and growth, and this theme will be expanded in the next chapter. God certainly has surprises in store for us, for the dialogue with African Traditional Religion may have consequences for the future shape of the Christian Church of which we now have no inkling.

To summarize the argument of this chapter, we may say that serious dialogue with African Traditional Religion is an essential condition for an African Christianity. This dialogue requires an encounter at the level of experience,

17

but it also requires the expertise needed to interpret the experience. Although formal dialogue will certainly take place at times with Non-Christians themselves, one of the most important, if not *the* most important area of encounter must be in the consciousness of the African Christian. Unless the Church becomes conscious at one and the same moment of the demands of both Christianity and the African Religions, Christianity in Africa is inviting syncretism. We have even gone so far as to say that syncretism is already more or less present in the African Church, and that this danger is all the more formidable because of present-day enthusiasm for adaptation and a positive approach to Non-Christian religions.

Notes

1. A very good discussion of the demands of dialogue and one on which this first paragraph is based is found in Howe, R. L., 1963, *The Miracle of Dialogue*, New York.

2. Prof. P. J. Rigby and Mr F. Lule made an unpublished study in 1972 of divination in peri-urban Kampala and discovered syncretism of the kind referred to here. I myself was asked to evaluate the Chwezi neo-traditional cult among Christians in Western Uganda in 1972.

3. Prof. Victor Turner has elaborated methods of analysing rituals. A summary of these is found in Shorter, A., 1972, 'Symbolism, Ritual and History, an Examination of the work of Victor Turner', in Ranger, T. O. and Kimambo, I. N., *The Historical Study of African Religion*, London, pp. 139-149.

4. Popper, K. R., 1945, *The Open Society and Its Enemies*, London.

5. *Nostra Aetate*, no. 2.

6. Wilson, M., 1959, *The Communal Rituals of the Nyakyusa*, Oxford, pp. 166-215.

7. Turner, V., 1968, *The Drums of Affliction*, Oxford.

8. Douglas, M., 1970, *Natural Symbols*, London, pp. vii-ix.

9. Cf. e.g. Shorter, A., 1970, 'The Migawo: Peripheral Spirit Possession and Christian Prejudice', *Anthropos*, Vol. 65, pp. 110-126.

10. Turner, H., 1965, 'A Typology for African Religious Movements', *Journal of Religion in Africa*, Vol. 1, Fasc. 3, pp. 1-34.

11. Cf. e.g. Swantz, M.-L., 1970, *Ritual and Symbol in Transitional Zaramo Society*, Uppsala, p. 340.

12. Tanner, R. E. S., 1968, 'Extempore Prayer among Adolescent Sukuma in Tanzania', *Nairobi Workshop in Religious Research*, pp. 391-396, (mimeographed).

13. Deniel, R., 1970, *Croyances Religieuses et Vie Quotidienne*, Paris-Ouagadougou, p. 299.

14. Turner, P., 1971, 'The Wisdom of the Ancestors and the Gospel of Christ: Some Notes on Christian Adaptation in Africa', *Journal of Religion in Africa*, Vol. 4, Fasc. 1, pp. 45-68.

15. Murphree, M. W., 1969, *Christianity and the Shona*, London, p. 2.

16. Zaehner, R. C., 1953, *Foolishness to the Greeks: An Inaugural Lecture*, Oxford, p. 22.

Chapter II

Africa's Contribution to World Christianity

1 African Christianity

The phrase 'African Christianity' gained a wide currency
after it was used by no less a person than Pope Paul VI. The
first Pan-African meeting of Roman Catholic Bishops had
just taken place at Gaba, Uganda, and it was Pope Paul
himself who closed the meeting with a speech in Rubaga
Cathedral, Kampala, on the first day of his historic visit to
Africa in 1969. During the course of his speech, the Pope
said this:

> The expression, that is, the language and mode of
> manifesting this one Faith may be manifold, hence it may
> be original, suited to the tongue, the style, the character,
> the genius and the culture of the one who professes this
> one Faith. From this point of view, a certain pluralism
> is not only legitimate, but desirable. An adaptation of
> the Christian life in the fields of pastoral, ritual, didactic
> and spiritual activities is not only possible, it is even
> favoured by the Church. The liturgical renewal is a living
> example of this. And in this sense you may, and you must,
> have an African Christianity. Indeed you possess human
> values and characteristic forms of culture which can rise
> up to perfection so as to find in Christianity, and for
> Christianity, a true superior fulness and prove to be capable
> of a richness of expression all its own, and genuinely
> African.[1]

The following year, at the second All-Africa Episcopal
Symposium, the hall of the University of Abidjan, Ivory
Coast, had been decorated with a huge banner bearing the
words: 'You may, and you must, have an African
Christianity.' Africa had taken the phrase to heart.

In the same speech at Kampala, Paul VI called this creation of an African Christianity 'an immense and original undertaking'. This was certainly no exaggeration. Finding 'in Christianity, and for Christianity, a true superior fulness' means asking the African Church to make a contribution to Christianity at world level, adding to the richness of the Church's universal and unfolding experience. As early as 1956 Robert Sastre made the same point, an African priest writing about liturgical adaptation:

> Adaptation is not particularization of the universal, if I may refer to it thus, but the elevation of the particular to a universal resonance. Particularism would mean finding value only in what originates from oneself or one's own people. Alienation, on the other hand, is to be incapable of finding among one's own people anything that could possibly have a universal vocation.[2]

These were very wise words, but they were also very exacting. Like the words of Pope Paul, they were a call for originality and originality cannot be produced to order, like a rabbit out of a hat. It is like telling a young and inexperienced artist to go and paint the Sistine Chapel. In other words, African Christians must realize that they are Fathers of a Church and founders of a tradition, before an African Christianity can become a reality.

Originality and genius are rare commodities at the best of times, but at the present juncture the African would-be Michelangelos are beset by a number of obstacles and pitfalls, even when they have been spotted by the talent scouts and convinced of their mission. A fundamental problem is the one referred to in the last chapter, the temptation of taking sides. The most important thing that should be said about African Christianity is that it is Christian. It is not enough to be African, for this is to fall into the pitfall of particularism in one of the forms we have identified, either syncretism or the closed system. On the other hand, there is the very real danger, referred to by Sastre, of alienation. The Church in Africa is being prevented from carrying out a conscious dialogue with African religious traditions because it is shackled by alien structures. It is prevented from becoming officially aware of its own identity and of the currents beneath its surface because an equation has been made between 'universal' and 'western'. The Pope is 'Patriarch of the West' and the Christianity that has been brought to Africa is almost wholly the Christianity professed by the 'Western Church'. While one can agree with Christopher Dawson that Western Europe has in part acquired the energy to transform the world from the spirit of Christianity which strives to incorporate itself in humanity and 'renew the face of the earth', one cannot include colonization, the spread of western capitalism, and the imposition of western language and culture in this movement of Christian world renewal. Western Christianity can be allowed to be a catalyst; it should not be an instrument of political, economic or cultural domination.

It is easy to pay lip-service to a religious ideal that combines the aspects of unity and diversity and which sees as one of its tasks that of helping individuals and nations to become more truly and completely themselves. Since the Second Vatican Council and the Uppsala Assembly of the World Council of Churches fine things have been said and written in this vein. Yet in spite of it all, African Christians remain in the shackles of a 'White Church', in the grip of forces that are not of their own making. A Church has been created in Africa which can only be sustained in strict bondage—organizational, cultural and financial—to the white world. The problem is how to end what Meinrad Hegba has called 'this state of eternal juniority'.[3]

> Nevertheless, one fear remains: historic Christianity bears so universally the imprint of the genius of other races, and Negritude ... insists so firmly on the official recognition of its own authenticity, that *de facto* we may always remain 'strangers and exiles', objects of charity to the 'citizens of heaven' and the 'servants of God'.[4]

Until there is a place in the World Church for an African Theology, for African Rites and for church structures of African inspiration, an African Christianity will never be a reality. The time will only come when we have stopped talking about translating Western Christianity into African terms, and have begun talking about translating African Christian ideas into western terms. It is not enough to

Africanize Christianity. African Christianity must discover a Catholic vocation.

2 African Philosophy

Although, in English-speaking Africa, Protestant writers have apparently been quicker to interest themselves in the religious beliefs of Traditional Africa than Catholic writers, their theology of religions seems to be developing at a slower pace. The first General Assembly of the All-Africa Conference of Churches at Kampala in 1963 was ultra-cautious. 'Traditional African culture,' it declared, 'was not all bad; neither was everything good.'[5] Six years later at Abidjan a very different statement was made, one which was both balanced and forward-looking:

> African Theology is 'a theology based on the Biblical faith of Africans, and which speaks to the African soul. It is expressed in categories of thought which arise out of the philosophy of the African people. This does not mean it is narrow in outlook (syncretistic). To speak of African Theology involves formulating clearly a Christian attitude to other religions. . . .'[6]

In spite of the hopes engendered by this statement, John Mbiti, writing in 1971, is by no means clear about the possibility of African Traditional Religion making a contribution to Christian Theology. Enthusiastic as he is for a theology of the living African Church, he nevertheless asks himself: '. . . how far can we, or should we, regard African religiosity as a *praeparatio evangelica*?'. The most he can say for the present is that the study of African Traditional Religion is 'a background which cannot be ignored'.[7] E. Bolaji Idowu is equally hesitant. For him, theologians must 'apprehend African spiritual values with the African mind while, at the same time, they possess the requisite knowledge of the fundamental facts of the faith which they are seeking to express and disseminate in indigenous idiom'.[8] He does not offer any opinions as to how the bearing in mind of African spiritual values will affect the idiom of Christianity in practice.

Discussion among both Catholic and Protestant writers has been held up by the assumption of a global approach to

23

the whole of sub-Saharan Africa, but among Catholic writers in English, it has been especially delayed by a preoccupation with philosophy. With their neo-scholastic training, Catholics assumed that there could be no African Theology without the prior discovery of an African Philosophy and the search for such a philosophy has met with disappointing results. Protestants, on the other hand, took a much more breezy attitude towards philosophy and refused to be distracted by it. John Mbiti paints a picture of religious diversity in traditional Africa, of many religious systems with similarities and differences. Underlying them, however, there is—he believes—a single philosophy, but he adds a note of caution:

> Philosophy of one kind or another is behind the thinking and acting of every people, and a study of traditional religions brings us into those areas of African life where, through word and action, we may be able to discern the philosophy behind. This involves interpretation of the information before us, and interpretation cannot be completely free of subjective judgement. What, therefore, is 'African Philosophy', may not amount to more than simply my own process of philosophizing the items under consideration: but this cannot be helped, and in any case I am by birth an African.[9]

The African neo-scholastic could hardly be satisfied with such a subjective approach to philosophy. His aim was to build a rational, conceptual system out of African traditional thought, a system comparable to those of western philosophy. Indeed, Alexis Kagamé, one of the foremost African philosophers, was honest enough to admit that without European Philosophy the question of an African Philosophy would never arise at all. It is only because he is inspired by European Philosophy that the African thinks of trying to express the traditional thought of his people as a conceptual system, and Kagamé, in particular, accepts Aristotle as his guide because he believes that this philosopher has a universal breadth and relevance.

Africans were at first flattered by an approach that took their original ideas seriously enough to build a rational, conceptual system out of them. They strongly resented the idea associated (not wholly justifiably) with the name of

Lévy-Bruhl that non-westerners were incapable of conceptualized thought, and they welcomed the prospect of an African (or sometimes a 'Bantu') Philosophy. The work of Placide Tempels and of his pupil, Alexis Kagamé, generated considerable and well-merited excitement in the 1940s and '50s.[10] With Aristotle and Aquinas as guides, rather than masters, they explored the abstract ideas of certain Bantu languages. They studied the African parallels of concepts beloved of the European philosophers: being, existence, and causality, or they constructed European-type systems on African key-concepts such as 'vital force'. In doing this, they certainly revealed new, and typically African, emphases and categories.

The eventual rejection of these pioneering, philosophical attempts as a 'dialectical contamination' was at least partly just, even if a trifle unkind.[11] These philosophical constructs were based almost exclusively on linguistic analyses, on language structure and on the range of meaning of particular words. The favoured literary source was the corpus of proverbs, commonly assumed to contain the wisdom of the African, and sometimes the names and attributes of the supreme being. In point of fact, proverbs are statements—often highly cynical statements—about life, that remain purely at the level of observation and experience; while the etymology of names, unsupported by any appeal to other kinds of evidence, can encourage all kinds of suppositions and fantasies, such as that perpetrated by Fridolin Bosch in his Yahwistic and Thomistic etymology of the Nyamwezi divine name, *Likube*. This he derives from the verb 'to be', *kubi*, making it mean 'the One who is'.[12] Needless to say, such an interpretation is rejected by the linguists.

The trouble with 'Bantu Philosophy' is that it represented a kind of demythologization of African symbolism. If it really deals with African concepts, it does not deal with them in an African way, and the model erected to discern these concepts usurps the place of traditional, symbolic structures of thought. Okot p'Bitek is right to say that it is a 'blind alley'. He also rightly condemns the facile dismissal of African forms of expression.

It is, to say the least, an unhelpful conceit to start off by holding that a people do not know what they believe, or cannot express it; and that it is the student—who, after all, is the ignorant person—who will tell the people what they believe. It seems to me that the role of the student of traditional religion and philosophy is, as it were, to photograph, in as much detail as possible, the way of life of the people; and then to make comments, pointing out the connexions and relevances of the different parts, and their ultimate relation to the whole of life.[13]

Part of the problem is the disdain which the professional philosopher used to feel for symbolic thought as something 'primitive' and lacking the cogency of reasoning. It was felt that symbols could not be studied systematically as symbols, but had to be translated into reasoned concepts, and that every people in the world had to evolve from a symbolic stage of thinking into a philosophical or scientific stage. The work of Claude Lévi-Strauss and the application of his methods to African material revealed that the structural analysis of symbols was possible, and that, while remaining in the sphere of rational science, the scholar—so far from doing violence to the concrete symbols—was actually articulating them and rendering them more intelligible.

However, as we noted in the last chapter, to restrict the analysis to verbal symbols only is no less dangerous than to restrict it to one literary genre. Symbolic action is as important as—even, more important than—oral symbolism for the communication of ideas, and here the work of Victor Turner in Zambia has proved of great value in complementing that of Lévi-Strauss. African ritual is, as Turner shows, a configuration of manufactured symbols with varied structures and different levels of meaning, and the methods he proposes provide a concrete application of the general procedure outlined by Okot p'Bitek. Turner's concept of the 'positional meaning' of symbols, according to which they are linked to other relevant contexts in the whole range of culture, is only a little more specific than Okot's 'relevances of the different parts, and their ultimate relation to the whole of life'. If such a method of study is being proposed for African cultures and systems of thought, then the question arises: Can we not bypass the philosophical stage altogether, and situate our African Theology in the African life-context, adequately studied by these various techniques? African theologians are already sensing that the old search for an African Philosophy is leading them nowhere and that what they need is an anthropologically based theology not a philosophically based theology.

3 African Theology and Black Theology

There is always a tendency to think of theology in terms of systematic theology, the application of philosophy and discursive reasoning to religious truths. This, however, is to make theology dependent on philosophy. Basically, theology is no more than *theo-logia*, a speaking about God or the gods, and every religion and religion-based culture can be said to have a theology. This theology can be studied scientifically and its structure discerned by the scholar. As we have seen (in the first chapter) Christianity has to come to terms with the theologies and systems of beliefs of the religion-based cultures of Africa, if it is to be Africanized at all. Without such a dialogue Christianity would simply be living in a vacuum. Christianity, therefore, cannot afford to neglect African Theology. However, as J. K. Agbeti rightly points out,[14] a distinction must be drawn between an African or 'indigenized' Christian Theology and the Theology of African religions. Both are legitimate uses of the term 'African Theology', but in this chapter we are concerned with the first meaning, reserving the second use for the next chapter. In both instances one can ask whether African Theology is a single entity, and in both instances we shall be obliged to say that it is not. There is no reason why there should not be a plurality of African approaches to Christian Theology, corresponding to a plurality of African traditional theologies. As we shall argue in the next chapter, a methodology which treats African religious systems as a single, unified phenomenon is simply not faithful to the facts. At best, it can produce only a few vague generalities that could be predicated of any religion in the world. What we need from the African Theologians is not a statement of the obvious as if it was uniquely African, but rather those insights which are precious and original—even if they can only be identified in certain places and at certain times.

African Christian Theology, then, will correspond to a culturally fragmented Africa, albeit with many chains of possible comparison and actual, historical interaction. It will

27

be a theology suited to modern national cultures which are essentially poly-ethnic in character, striving to weld together into unity a variety of traditions. These national cultures are each developing in their own way as heirs of differing sets of interacting tribal cultures, and the theology which caters for these differing and complex experiences cannot be expected to be other than pluriform. In saying this, however, we are not denying the fact that in African tradition many elements, such as ideas of the supreme being, religious concepts of authority, rituals and so on, may transcend basic ethnic and cultural allegiances, but such facts must be demonstrated before they can be made the basis for general theological statements.

Some writers, such as Neckebrouck,[15] have a tendency to minimize the element of continuity between the theology of traditional African religions and indigenized Christian theology. For them it is preferable to speak of 'theology in Africa', rather than of 'African Theology'.[16] This approach is altogether too sceptical. It is perfectly true, as Neckebrouck points out, that we cannot expect an African Theology to solve the basic crisis of faith in God which the western world is currently experiencing, before Africa herself has experienced the same crisis. There are many indications that Africa is about to be confronted by problems of religious belief comparable to those of the west, but it is also quite probable that—with or without the help of western solutions —she will try to solve these problems in her own way. In the countries of independent Africa emotional support has been generated for the values and concepts of the traditional religion, so much so that they are becoming, in many cases, symbols of national or African identity. The 'authenticity' which is so fiercely proclaimed in Zaïre admits of other levels of intensity elsewhere.

It is natural that in South Africa where African culture has been used as the tool of white superiority for keeping the races apart and for frustrating African aspirations to modernity and higher living standards, Africans should be less fervent in promoting continuity with tradition. Political necessities appear more urgent to them than the need to cultivate a pride in their traditional heritage. Indeed, in sophisticated circles the integration of traditional values and modern aspirations may be so complete as to pass unnoticed, and many South African Blacks are not conscious of any unresolved duality in their make-up. Hence the impact in South Africa of the philosophy of 'Negritude' and of the Black-American concept of a Liberation Theology.[17] Theology in South Africa becomes—perhaps more than elsewhere in the continent—a situational theology which strives to confront crucial socio-political realities. In doing this, however, it cannot escape the ultimate requirement of a positive content. A man is not only liberated *from* something; he is liberated *for* something else. In this case the African is liberated to become—not a European, or a white South African—but to become more fully and truly himself, and in deciding what he is, he must become conscious of the values by which he lives, whether or not he recognizes their origin in his own tradition. A discerning critic, such as Bucher, is thus able to discover—even in the Black Theology of South Africa—certain themes which are typical of African tradition: the stress on the wholeness of life, an optimism that characterizes the man-centred cosmologies of Africa, an emphasis on communal salvation and the community between living and dead.[18] It can be readily seen, therefore, that, while an African Theology inherits concepts and values —consciously or unconsciously—from an authentic tradition of its own, it is far from being an antiquarian exercise, or an advocacy of a return to the past.

4 The Nature of Africa's Contribution

Bishop Sundkler once expressed the belief that an African Theology would be born 'in the act of preaching'.[19] It would only come about, he thought, when Africans were faced with the problem of re-interpreting the Christian message to their own people. There is considerable truth in the necessary link which Sundkler poses between theology and preaching, and in the value of an African re-interpretation of the Christian message, but experience of preaching in Africa belies the hope that it may become a source of African Theology. Preaching depends on two things if it is to be effective and creative. It must be close to the corpus of beliefs, the revealed message, and it must be close to the real concerns and needs of the congregation. All too frequently preaching fails on both counts, even in the churches of official Christian denominations, as opposed to those of independent movements.

The favoured themes of preachers are few and repetitious and sermons are frequently negative and moralizing. As in other parts of the world, the sermon has to compete with other, more effective, means of communication, and suffers by comparison. There is also small chance of preachers influencing one another and so reaching a consensus. It would seem therefore that the re-interpretation involved in preaching is secondary to an even more fundamental level of reinterpretation, a conscious reflection about the emerging values of modern African societies in the light of Christian revelation.

A more recent, and more acceptable, suggestion has been made several times that an African Theology will derive from an African reading of Scripture.[20] Clearly, if African theologians are to enjoy any originality, they must go themselves to the source of revelation, and must make the Word of God the key to their understanding of their own problems and priorities as Africans. This is to approach the question of an African Theology from the opposite end, and it presupposes a comprehensive knowledge of African human values. In other words, an African reading of the Bible must be an informed reading of the Bible.

For many people, Africans included, a theology which is African and which at the same time is making a contribution to the World Church is a contradiction in terms, although, in fact, the African Socialists and political philosophers have long ago discovered that it is only when Africa has a contribution to make at world level that she can be deemed to have any identity or originality. The Church, it is felt, is a different matter, being Catholic by nature and transcending the particular cultures in which her doctrines are expressed. It is vaguely imagined that there exists some pure form of Christianity, some basic raw material which has simply to be translated and handed round. At other times the dangers of theological pluralism are magnified as being a threat to the unity and integrity of the deposit of faith. Such objections arise from a static and unitary view of Christianity which sees the Truth as something appropriated by the Church in its entirety and perfection, instead of as a horizon towards which—in dialogue with other religious views—Christians are moving and growing. The one, basic and universal fact is Christ, revealing God to us, and being himself revealed as a historic man in Sacred Scripture. This man, however, is not encountered in the reading of a printed page. On the contrary, he is encountered, in virtue of the resurrection, in the lives of human individuals and communities, in the communication and continuity that exists between human groups in both space and time. This is the foundation for local schools of Christian Theology, and it is important not to rob the Church Universal of Africa's contribution by making theology in Africa simply a work of translation. There is no doubt that it is important for Africans to listen to European theologians and to translate their ideas into the terms of their own culture, but if it is admitted that the cultural formulation is secondary, there is absolutely no justification whatever for the process of translation going only one way. Indeed, as we shall now show, the very universality and integrity of the Christian message demands a balanced exchange.

The Church needs the African theological contribution for her own theological health. This contribution is not going to destroy or alter the universal tradition, but it may operate first of all as a corrective in a number of ways. Firstly, it may awaken themes in universal Christianity which are dormant, or latent. Secondly, it may help to show that certain elements presented to Africa as essential in the universal tradition are in fact secondary elements, deriving from the particular western cultural tradition. In addition to this corrective contribution, there should be a positive role for African theology. The World Church has to serve, to speak to, a world in which Africans and Blacks generally have an increasingly important voice. Africa is a fact to be reckoned with and the Church cannot afford not to enlist the services of African theologians to speak to this world. The universality of Christian Theology, therefore, turns out to be a developing universality, keeping pace with a world in evolution. African Theology will help the Church to open up new avenues for exploration, to develop a new awareness, in short, to cease to be a 'White Church'.

We are not in any way restricting the African theological contribution to the insights of the non-Christian religious traditions of Africa. As we have already said, theology must be contemporary and must derive from modern cultural life. Nevertheless, it would be a grave mistake to assume that

31

ancient religious ideas are not highly resilient in the modern situation. These ideas are often the last things to be affected by change, and they belong to the basic cultural coding of the individual. The fear is often expressed that an African Theology runs the risk of degenerating into syncretism, but, as we have already demonstrated, syncretism is a greater danger when there is no real communication or dialogue between religious systems. We have too much syncretism already, as it is, and this came about without the assistance of an African Theology.

The missionaries who proclaimed the Christian Good News for the first time in African countries did not, for the most part, ask themselves how their message was being understood. They assumed that the African peoples they were addressing employed the same thought categories as themselves. They also assumed that cultural translation was an easy task and that one could, for example, simply identify the Creator-God of the African religion with God the Father of Christian tradition. The result was what Tanner has called 'a working misunderstanding',[21] the juxtaposition of elements from differing systems. Whether this misunderstanding 'works' or not, depends on what one expects it to do, but misunderstanding means syncretism, not integration. African Christianity and African Theology cannot be based on a misunderstanding.

Africans feel the need for a real synthesis on Christian terms. At an unsophisticated level the synthesis is made by the independent churches, but it scarcely rises above the level of syncretism in most cases. Moreover, the fissiparous nature of these churches encourages an absolute pluralism which prevents their making a direct contribution to Christianity. Very often the existence itself of the independent churches is a protest against membership of a world-wide communion in which the African is condemned to silence. In the measure in which independent churches 'drop out' of universal Christianity, they become particularist and eventually despised by their African members, themselves. They stand, however, as a warning to Christians of the ancient communions of what happens when the synthesis is disallowed.

5 *The Content of Africa's Contribution*

So far we have been discussing the nature of Africa's contribution to World Christianity; nothing has been said about the content of this contribution. This is not surprising because the contribution cannot, by any stretch of the imagination, be said to have been made yet. We have already noted the interests of Black Theology in South Africa, and how these reveal certain traditional themes and concerns. It belongs, obviously, to African theologians themselves to say what their contribution is likely to contain, and at the moment it is virtually impossible to know what they think. Their theses lie scattered in the university libraries of Europe and America and nothing has been done to bring them together. It is perhaps unlikely that these works would reveal much homogeneity, or even originality. Their authors have not been able to influence one another. Few have been permitted to carry out original research in the field and many, if not most, have not been permitted to break free of European interpretations and styles. What we are waiting for is an independent and original contribution from Africa itself. There are signs that it is on the horizon and that it will proceed along the lines we have been discussing.

In the meantime of what value are the opinions of a European missionary observer? It is, of course, ridiculous to pretend that a European can identify completely with the African mentality, or even—as some anthropologists claimed to do—preserve a neutral position. Nevertheless, it is possible to be a 'marginal African'—to possess an attitude of mind which disposes one to be actively understanding and sympathetic to the African culture and to the aspirations of African Christians. This is not a passive role at all. Some writers suggest that there is a partial or even near-total rejection of missionaries by their African colleagues and that the renewal of the Church of which missionaries are the exponents is seen as an attempted come-back to power, and therefore a threat to African autonomy. There is some truth in the suggestion, but there are also signs that missionaries are helping Africans to be convinced that the renewal is in their own hands. There are signs also that expatriate missionaries are being accepted as collaborators, possessed of enough African experience to be allowed to speak with their African colleagues to the world. What is said here about the possible content of an African Theology must be accepted in this spirit.

The first area in which Africa can probably make a contribution is in the realm of the so-called 'secular theology'. Secularism is often wrongly assumed to be the final phase in an evolutionary movement towards a more developed technology, but it has nothing inherently to do with modern living or with the scientific discoveries of our age. As Mary Douglas points out, secularism is the 'product of definable social experience',[22] and it is possible to point to traditional African societies with a secular emphasis in their outlook. The more common experience of Africa has been the religious outlook, but one that was fully integrated with every aspect of individual and social life. This integration was so far-reaching that some scholars have concluded that African traditional religion was vitiated by being world-centred and pragmatic.[23] This view probably reflects a western dichotomy between sacred and profane, spirit and matter, supernatural and natural. In these days, when we are abandoning such an exaggerated dualism, it is easier to accept that Africans are focused upon a world which is both spiritual and material at the same time. *Pace* Neckebrouck, it may be that African theologians could help the world rediscover the relativity of such terms as 'sacred' and 'profane' and encourage the typically African vision of 'wholeness' or integration.

Several other possible themes are really aspects of this first one. An important one is the emphasis on conscious symbolism as a means of communication. Symbolism is central to an integrated and balanced view of reality. It is an appeal to experience, and at the same time an appeal to the meaning which underlies the experience. Symbolism is the means by which the spheres of sacred and secular are bridged, by which the sacred is spoken of in secular terms. The western world has been experiencing a contempt for symbolism because it has inherited a forest of symbols that no longer refer to modern life as it is lived, or to any fundamental human experience. The temptation is there to conceptualize all symbols because of the prestige of scientific rationalization. This is a characteristic symptom of western secularism. When all the symbols have gone, one is left without an intuition of the sacred. Western man, mankind as a whole, needs to regain respect for symbolism.

Another theme is that of fecundity. Africans place great value on physical generation, on life and the sharing of life. Fundamentally this is because of their humanity and their esteem for inter-personal relationships. In the western world 'the good life' has been equated with mechanical ingenuity, with labour-saving devices, with the easier and cheaper manufacture of household goods and luxuries. Such an equation is ultimately dehumanizing. It is no progress to exalt mechanical ingenuity over personal values. If technology is in itself a good thing and a means of sharing in the creativity of God, then personal values must be preserved in a technologically developed world. Africa has not yet felt the full impact of western technology. Perhaps she may never be as heavily industrialized and urbanized as other parts of the world. On the other hand, even in the rural areas, she is feeling the effects of a profound social revolution. Perhaps Africans may be no more successful than westerners in preventing a technological society from becoming an impersonal and an enslaved one. On the other hand, with so much emphasis on the value of the human person, African theologians might assist in a process of revaluation.

Bound up with the theme of fecundity is that of 'man-in-community', a theme illustrated by Pope Paul VI in his letter to Africa of 1967. According to the Pope it has three characteristics, the spiritual view of life, the sense of family and the sense of community. We are now quite familiar with the idea of 'man-in-community' from the political philosophy of Senghor, Nyerere, Kaunda and so many others. The assumption is that man only discovers his full personality in group relationships. Man-in-community is, as Mboya wrote, 'both an end and an entity'.[24] Africa understands very well the nature of community, the freedom of the individual within the community, and the responsibility of the individual for the community. Very closely related to 'man-in-community' is what Turner calls 'liminality', the condition ascribed to a group of African initiants undergoing a rite of passage from one state of life to another.[25] In this state they discover the deep springs of their humanity and hold up to society a mirror in which are reflected its most cherished values.

Africa has much to teach the world about friendship in the community. Its characteristic mental process, the extrapolation of ideas, which illustrates African extroversion, is another fruitful ground for exploration. Finally, there is very wide agreement about the priority of a theology of relationships between human and spiritual beings, particularly between the living and dead. This is a strong preoccupation of traditional religious systems in Africa and it could possibly provide an enrichment for the Christian idea of the Communion of Saints.

There is obviously a vast theological potential in Africa, not simply in spite of contemporary change, but because of it. It is no good our wringing our hands over the passing world of traditional Africa. That would be naïve. But it would be an even graver sin to imagine that the African is condemned to be a passive observer of all that is taking place in his continent, or that he simply wants to ape western ways of life forever. Political philosophers, writers and poets are already looking for elements of continuity with tradition which will enable them to interpret the modern world according to the African genius. Is it too much to hope that African theologians are following in their wake?

Notes

1. Paul VI, 1969, 'Closing Discourse to All-Africa Symposium', *Gaba Pastoral Paper No. 7*, pp. 50-51.

2. Sastre, R., 1957, 'Liturgie Romaine et Négritude', in *Des Prêtres Noirs s'Interrogent*, Paris, p. 163.

3. Hegba, M., n.d., *Personnalité Africaine et Catholicisme*, Paris, p. 14.

4. Hegba, M., 1957, 'Christianisme et Négritude', in *Des Prêtres Noirs s'Interrogent*, Paris, pp. 199-200.

5. AACC, 1963, *Drumbeats from Kampala*, London.

6. AACC, 1969, *Engagement*, Nairobi.

7. Mbiti, J., 1971, *New Testament Eschatology in an African Background*, Oxford, pp. 189-190.

8. Idowu, E. B., 1973, *African Traditional Religion, A Definition*, London, p. xi.

9. Mbiti, J., 1969, *African Religions and Philosophy*, London, pp. 1-2.

10. Tempels, P., 1959, *Bantu Philosophy*, Paris; Kagamé, A., 1955, *La Philosophie Bantu-Rwandaise de l'Etre*, Brussels.

11. Howlett, J., 1949, in *Présence Africaine*, Paris, p. 7.

12. Cf. Schönenberger, P., 1961, 'Names for God Known and Used by the Nyamwezi', *Anthropos*, Vol. 56, fasc. 5/6, pp. 947-949.

13. Okot p'Bitek, 1973, *Africa's Cultural Revolution*, 1973, pp. 62-63.

14. Agbeti, J. K., 1972, 'African Theology: What it is', in *Presence*, Vol. 5, no. 3, p. 7.

15. Neckebrouck, V., 1971, *L'Afrique Noire et La Crise Religieuse de l'Occident*, Tabora.

16. *Ibid.*, p. 253.

17. Motlabi, M., (ed.), 1972, *Essays on Black Theology*, Johannesburg, 1973.

18. Bucher, H., 1973, 'Black Theology in South Africa', *African Ecclesiastical Review*, Vol. 15, no. 4, pp. 329-339.

19. Sundkler, B., 1960, *The Christian Ministry in Africa*, London, p. 103.

20. Cf. AACC, 1969, *Engagement*, Nairobi, and Riches, P., 1971, 'Towards an African Theology', *Sharing*, May, Vol. 3, no. 4, pp. 5-6.

21. Tanner, R. E. S., 1967, *Transition in African Beliefs*, New York, p. 122.

22. Douglas, M., 1970, *Natural Symbols*, London, p. ix.

23. E.g. Mbiti, J., 1969, *African Religions and Philosophy*, London, pp. 4-5. Mbiti makes a distinction, however, between religiosity and philosophy. It is the former that he is criticizing here.

24. Mboya, T., 1964, *Freedom and After*, London, pp. 163 ff.

25. Turner, V., 1969, *The Ritual Process*, London, pp. 94-130.

Chapter III

The Comparative Study of African Religion

1 Introduction to the Problem

The Kimbu, in common with other peoples of western Tanzania, believe in the existence of a spirit that lives in the surrounding woodland wilderness and who controls the movements of the wild animals. He is called *Idimungala* in the Kimbu tradition and he constitutes one of the many versions of the Master of the Animals, a familiar figure in African societies where hunting is a specialization. *Idimungala* is a giant with many heads and when a lone traveller or huntsman encounters him on the path he loses all sense of direction and becomes lost in the bush. The Kimbu customarily attribute disappearances to the Master of the Animals and most accidents and wanderings in the forest are thought to be caused by him.

To many people the study of African religions must seem like an encounter with *Idimungala*! Religion in Africa is a many-headed giant and the unwary scholar can easily lose all sense of direction when he beholds all those heads and eyes and mouths. After years of study and research by innumerable scholars no methodology has emerged which allows us to view African Traditional Religion as a convincing unity. It is, perhaps, for this reason that African Traditional Religion has never been placed on a par by theologians and ecumenists with the so-called 'world religions'. During the debate in the Second Vatican Council on the Declaration on the Relationship of the Church to Non-Christian Religions (*Nostra Aetate*), Bishops from Africa and scholars like Cardinal Koenig asked for a mention in the document of the African Religions.[1] It was decided, however, to restrict the mention of Non-Christian religions to the traditional idea of great religions of the world, Hinduism, Buddhism, Judaism and Islam. In the same way, a comparable discrimination was displayed by the Anglican scholar of religion, Bishop Stephen Neill, in a discussion of the dialogue of Christianity with other religions. In a chapter entitled 'The Primitive World' he makes the damning statement:

> If we are prepared to understand religion in terms of a man's total reaction to the totality of life, we may be led to regard the primitive peoples as among the most religious people on earth. If, on the other hand, we look for certain signs or ideas of higher religion, we may deny to them almost any religion at all.[2]

Complexity, particularism, rural conditions, poorly developed material culture, absence of written literature—all these are factors contributing to adverse judgement upon African Religions, the judgement that they are devoid of 'ideas of higher religion'. Without an adequate methodology the riches of African Religion cannot be revealed and the scholar is tempted to despise the little he can see. Anyone, however, who has succeeded in overcoming the obstacles and who has been confronted in dialogue with the essential meanings and values of African Traditional Religions will know that they are capable of the highest religious purposes and intuitions. The question of methodology, therefore, looms large if there is to be any meeting between Christianity and African Religion.

2 The Particularist Approach

The classical approach of the social anthropologist to African religion and society is fiercely particularist, insisting on a thorough-going study in each and every ethnic group, and professing an almost total agnosticism in respect of any similarities or links between them. This attitude was encouraged both by the nature of African societies themselves and by the development of the discipline in response to its object of study. African tribes enjoyed their own political autonomy in pre-colonial days, they were culturally and linguistically isolated from each other to a greater or lesser degree, and they made their own, independent adaptations to different or similar environments. It was obvious that the study of African society had to begin with these basic units of social identity and ideology. Confronted with this situation social anthropology adopted an understandable and—indeed —a highly productive, holism. The social facts of African peoples, religion included, were studied in the light of integrating theories or structures which anthropologists believed they could discern in the cultures of those concerned. The result has been a series of penetrating studies, revealing a whole new world of unfamiliar values and ways of thinking which has enabled Africa to make her contribution to the culture of mankind as a whole. All of this has been an unparalleled enrichment, but it cannot be allowed to rest there, as if there were no further peaks for social anthropologists to scale.

The first generation of field-working anthropologists, absorbed by their discoveries, were not prepared to take any step towards a systematic comparison between ethnic groups. All such attempts they rejected or else relegated to a remote and unforeseeable future. Little by little, however, they and their successors were forced to come to terms with comparison, and the dilemma is aptly illustrated by the evolution of a series such as that of the *Ethnographic Survey of Africa* pioneered by the International African Institute. This series was described by its initiator and general editor as 'a series of separate, self-contained studies, each devoted to one particular people or cluster of peoples'.[3] The heart of the problem lies in the interpretation of the word 'cluster'. According to what criteria, it can be asked, are people judged to form a cluster? Are they simply criteria of geographical contiguity or linguistic affinity, or are the peoples concerned deemed to constitute a homogeneous, cultural unity? This was a problem that the series never resolved, and in its self-confessed incompleteness and tentativeness it produced many different approaches and answers, although it had started on the assumption that each study would be 'self-contained' and 'particular'.

The particularism and static relativism of traditional social anthropology has been reinforced in recent years by the ethnicity of African scholars themselves. Such scholars justifiably repudiate the superficiality and misapprehensions of some European and American anthropologists, and, in the name of serious scholarship, demand that particular studies be carried out only by qualified members of the ethnic group in question. For example, Prof. E. B. Idowu writes:

> The more limited the area covered, the more effective and honest the study will be. No honest scholar can be quite satisfied with a study done by proxy through research assistants scattered all over the field or by library work, whereas there is no way of avoiding either of these methods where the area covered is large and the scholar himself does not understand more than one or two of the languages. As the study must go on until enough scholars are produced all over Africa to tackle the subject each in his own language area, any study done in such areas where the native tongue is not that of the scholar must be regarded as tentative.[4]

This short passage contains a number of important but arguable ideas. No one will disagree that serious scholarship is required and that thorough-going research must be carried out by people fully conversant with the language of those they study. On the other hand, all science is tentative, setting up, testing, demolishing or correcting hypotheses. Studies carried out at different periods in the history of a discipline reflect different hypotheses and comparison may be rendered difficult by the particular interests and prejudices of the scholar himself, even when he comes from the ethnic group under study. Obviously, too, fluency in the language is an immense advantage to the scholar, but much also depends on his own status in the society. In many cases the participant observation of the indigenous scholar may be more credible and easier of acceptance; in other cases, however, the 'honoured stranger' or 'outsider' is accepted more readily and trusted more fully than the 'home-boy'. In any case, it is at the moment far beyond the bounds of practicality to find an indigenous scholar of religion for every African ethnic group. As David Barrett pointed out, there are over one hundred thousand names, alternative names and variant spellings for African ethnic groups, and even if one accepts G. P. Murdock's criteria of selection, one is still left with 853 'tribes' to be studied in the African continent.[5] We shall obviously have to wait a long time for the needed 853 African scholars of religion to make their appearance, and when they do, the work of comparative analysis will still entail library work and the reliance on the researches of others. It is important, however, that the primary resources should be reliable, for without competent groundwork comparison is ultimately impossible. It is equally important that comparison should be carried out by scholars who have experienced such primary fieldwork at first hand, so that they are aware of the problems and understand the kind of material they are handling.

However, the picture is not quite so simple as it has been painted so far. It is a fallacy to imagine a two-stage process in which scholars first of all do the necessary groundwork and then turn their attention to comparative analysis. Comparative analysis must, in the nature of things, accompany even the groundwork itself. A completely particularist stage is not true to the facts, since every ethnic group is as much a category of interaction with other groups as a self-contained, inward looking unit. The particularist approach, whether it is relative or absolute, overlooks the fact that, while particular ethnic groups enjoyed political autonomy in the past and an economy that was mainly self-sufficient, other aspects of culture—especially those in the sphere of religious belief and practice—were often widely shared with neighbouring groups. Moreover, history reveals these ethnic groups as developing, changing, coalescing, shrinking and disappearing over the years. They neither were, nor are, static phenomena. Today, competent field studies must take the historical dimension into account. They must also come to terms, to however small an extent, with the mass of competent particular studies which have already appeared. So much good work has already been done that it would be foolish to ignore it, and unwise to assume that it cannot be examined intelligently on a broader plane. Today, the world of scholarship demands more than the isolated monograph or even the symposium of particular studies.

3 The Enumerative Approach

The enumerative approach is what its name implies—the simple enumeration of different items, traditions, beliefs and practices. Scholars have adopted this approach because they feel that strict, comparative analysis is either impossible or not worthwhile. Geoffrey Parrinder is an outstanding example of this point of view. He writes:

> The study of ancient traditional religious beliefs of Africa is doubly difficult. First, there is the great variety and multiplicity of peoples, the lack of a central tradition, especially in Africa south of the Sahara. This can be overcome to some extent, by selecting beliefs of outstanding importance shared by different peoples, while noting regional differences; but it must be recognized that this is only partial and many exceptions may remain unobserved. However, the effort must be made, because the only alternative is to abandon the study altogether. The second difficulty is the complete lack of written documents from within the religion.[6]

What Parrinder is saying here is that the only possible method for studying African religions is that of enumerating 'beliefs of outstanding importance', even though these beliefs are subject to regional differences and are not completely comparable. Parrinder has in fact, like all genuine scholars, undergone a development in his thinking. The approach indicated by the above passage is infinitely more cautious than that of his earlier work. Fifteen years earlier he could write:

> [The] great comparative homogeneity of African society is apparent in the religious sphere ... in religious beliefs there is a great similarity between many parts of the continent that cuts across racial origins perhaps because of contacts over the centuries.... We shall try then to treat African religion on a comparative basis, gathering material from various parts of the continent.[7]

In fact, Parrinder's intuition that similarity between different religious traditions in the African continent is due to contacts over the centuries is largely correct, but his earlier comparative method is vitiated by his historical 'agnosticism'. African religions have a long history, but, in his view, the absence of written texts means that we cannot know it. Comparability must simply be assumed. In his later work he is more aware of the dangers of such an assumption, but he is still sceptical of oral history.

> The history of the traditional religion is unknown and few foreign descriptions were made before this century that merit close study, though there are a few hints in some of the more careful explorers' writings. This means that the development of religion can rarely be guessed....[8]

Rejecting, as he does, the historical study of African religion, Parrinder is led to abandon his earlier incautious comparison and to replace it with an approach that is more enumerative in character.

An enumerator has to group his material in one way or another, and if he is playing down the possibility of comparison he cannot afford to be too specific about his categories. It is interesting, in this connection, to note the difference between the headings used by Parrinder in 1954 and in 1969. The earlier work included headings such as: 'Nature Gods', 'Ancestors', 'Divine Rulers', 'The Soul and its Destiny'. The later work has: 'Philosophy and Cosmology', 'Ritual Word and Action', 'Society and Morals'.[9] The development is towards larger and more general categories. Without effective comparison, the enumerator must either use categories that are precise but alien to the material he is describing, or that are so general that they have no real meaning. To go in for chapter headings, as many authors do, such as 'the Soul', 'the After-Life', 'Sin', etc. is begging the question whether and how such concepts are to be found in traditional religions.[10]

The classic enumerator of all time was Sir James Frazer, author of *The Golden Bough*.[11] Frazer enumerated endless 'litanies' of facts gathered from every age, country and social group. Vaulting lightly from one continent to another, across immense distances of space and time, he passed from one belief or practice to another, linked only by a superficial similarity observed by himself. The modern neo-Frazerian gives the master credit for his assumption that all men are intellectuals, capable of empirical and reasoned thought, and for the attempt at a rational cultural translation, but, in so far as it fails to situate the facts it studies in whole contexts, the Frazerian approach is sterile and its 'litanies' are devoid of meaning. The enumerator, therefore, stands on the horns of a dilemma: either to go in for undeclared and unsubstantiated comparisons, or to produce a 'telephone directory' of unconnected items.

One type of enumeration that is less objectionable is the symposium of particular studies, each representing a different aspect or category. Thus, one study might treat of the Supreme Being, another of Sacrifice, another of Priesthood and so on. Each study is valid in itself, but the juxtaposition of the different studies might give the false impression that each case is a paradigm for the aspect in question on a continental scale, and that the whole collection provides a complete picture of religion in Africa as a whole. The Symposium edited by Kwesi Dickson and Paul Ellingworth (*Biblical Revelation and African Beliefs*, London 1969) is in fact, more complex than this, employing in its various contributions, a number of different methods and approaches. By and large, however, the different authors write about their subject with special reference to an ethnic group that they themselves know well. This by no means prejudices the value of what they write; it is merely that the reader must clearly understand the nature of the material he is handling. Enumeration is always an invitation to make comparisons and it can rarely resist doing so. For this reason the various comparative approaches are more common and it is to them that we turn now.

4 *The Hypothesis of Unity Approach*

A fundamental question is whether comparability can be assumed or whether it must be demonstrated before the scholar can go ahead and make the comparisons. For many writers the assumption of comparability is acceptable and this allows them to take the short cut to comparison. Everything depends upon the hypothesis that a basic cultural unity exists in Africa south of the Sahara, and the authors place their faith in this premise of unity. The two major criticisms of such a method are: firstly, that the hypothesis takes as many different forms as there are scholars, and secondly, that the hypothesis, whatever form it takes, remains unproven and is, in fact, incapable of proof by its very nature.

One of the most subtle examples of the hypothesis of unity approach is provided by Professor W. E. Abraham, the

Ghanaian philosopher. Abraham introduces the notion of the paradigm or 'family resemblance'.

> The resemblances between cultures of the same type are rather to be thought of in terms of family likeness. Here the same culture could markedly resemble different cultures of the same type in different ways—like the members of a family. This is what justifies the substantial treatment of an individual culture treated as paradigmatic of a type. It would be unsatisfactory to attempt to present the schema of the type itself.[12]

Abraham, therefore, declares his faith in the 'family likeness' of African cultures, but absolves himself of the necessity of proving that such a likeness exists. He is not, in fact, making comparisons, but is simply stating his belief that in treating one African culture—the culture of the Akan peoples of Ghana—he is saying something about all African cultures. The title of his book, *The Mind of Africa*, reflects this claim.

For Professor John Mbiti there are many African religions, and he sets himself the task of collecting and comparing their different beliefs and practices because, in his view, they all subscribe to a single, basic, religious philosophy.

> While religion can be discerned in terms of beliefs, ceremonies, rituals and religious officiants, philosophy is not so easily distinguishable. We shall consider different religions in terms of their similarities and differences, to give us a picture of the overall situation in Africa. But, since there are no parallel philosophical systems which can be observed in similarly concrete terms, we shall use the singular, 'philosophy', to refer to the philosophical understanding of African peoples concerning different issues of life.[13]

Mbiti concentrates, therefore, on the 'concrete' expressions of African religions, very frankly admitting that the religious philosophy behind them is an interpretation which (as we have seen in the previous chapter) 'cannot be completely free of subjective judgement'.[14]

Canon J. V. Taylor is, perhaps, even more frankly subjective than Professor Mbiti. He asks:

46

But is it possible to speak of African Religion as if it were one and the same throughout the continent south of the Sahara? Certainly there is not one homogeneous system of belief throughout Africa. One tribe gives prominence to an element which is only vaguely conceived in another. In several ways the traditional culture of the whole Niger basin reveals a sophistication and an individuation that is not known elsewhere. Nevertheless anyone who has read a number of ethnological works dealing with different parts of Africa must be struck not only by the remarkable number of features that are common but by the emergence of a basic world-view which fundamentally is everywhere the same. To quote an Akan proverb, Man's one speech has thirty varieties but they are slight.[15]

In this passage, Taylor goes so far as to posit the existence of a 'basic world-view' in African religion as well as of 'features that are common'. He does not, however, offer a clear outline of this world-view, or of how the various features of African religion which he treats so sympathetically in the succeeding chapters form an integrated whole.

We have already seen that Professor E. B. Idowu rightly calls for a thorough-going research in each and every culture region, although we have ventured to differ from him in his recommendation of a postponement of systematic comparison. Idowu believes that all comparative analysis must be tentative until the groundwork has been done by indigenous scholars. In the meantime, however, he declares his faith in a 'common factor' or 'common Africanness' uniting the different religious systems.

When we look at Africa with reference to beliefs, our first impression is of certain objective phenomena which appear to be made up of systems of beliefs and practices which are unrelated except in so far as they are loosely held together by the factors of common localities and languages. But a careful look, through actual observation and comparative discussions with Africans from various parts of the continent, will show, first and foremost, that there is a common factor which the coined word *négritude* will express aptly. There is a common Africanness about the total culture and religious beliefs and practices of Africa. This common factor may be due either to the fact of diffusion or to the fact that most Africans share common origins with regard to race and customs and religious practices.[16]

With this tentative hypothesis, Idowu is able to plunge into comparisons between a variety of African religious systems on a continental scale.

Idowu is quite right to admit that the hypothesis of unity is unproven—that it is, in fact, a hypothesis and nothing else. In his case it is supported by 'actual observation and comparative discussions with Africans from various parts of the continent'.[17] In the case of Taylor it is based on the impression gained from reading 'a number of ethnological works dealing with different parts of Africa'.[18] For Mbiti the hypothesis is supported by his own philosophizing. As he writes in all honesty, 'What, therefore, is "African Philosophy", may not amount to more than simply my own process of philosophizing the items under consideration: but this cannot be helped, and in any case I am by birth an African'.[19] For Abraham, 'it would be unsatisfactory to attempt to present the schema of the type itself'.[20] The existence of the type is therefore simply asserted, without being either demonstrated or even described. The proponents of the hypothesis of unity approach are well aware of its failings, but the question is whether they are right to assume that nothing more than this can be done.

5 *The Historical Approach*

It is one thing to say that we are not able to know African history; quite another to say that Africa has no history worth recording. Generally speaking modern writers, who reject the historical approach, are of the former opinion, rather than the latter. 'Each African people has its own history',[21] writes Professor Mbiti. The question is: Can we know it? Dr Parrinder's answer is unequivocal: 'The history of the traditional religion is unknown ...'[22] and this opinion rests on Parrinder's own scepticism about the value of oral methods of historical research. John Mbiti's scepticism is in many ways more fundamental, and he has even been accused by Professors Kimambo and Ranger of propounding an African religious philosophy that is 'anti-historical'.[23] According to Mbiti, African traditional religions have no founders, no reformers, no missionaries and no converts,[24] but more important still, Africans have a concept of time that prevents them from knowing what their history is. Africans, Mbiti tells us, do not have a historical view of the world. Beyond the experienced past is the macro-time period referred to by the Swahili word *zamani*.

> *Zamani* is the graveyard of time, the period of termination, the dimension in which everything finds its halting point. It is the final storehouse for all phenomena and events, the ocean of time in which everything becomes absorbed into a reality that is neither after nor before.[25]

This macro-time period, here described with such poetic feeling, is, we are told, the source and pattern for all the African's actions and decisions in the modern situation, but it is not susceptible of strict historical analysis. It is too dominated by myth and uncertainty. Mbiti believes that something of African religious history can be salvaged by the interdisciplinary co-operation of historians, anthropologists and theologians, but he also believes that our knowledge is too incomplete for a worthwhile attempt to be made at the present time. Writing in 1969, he says:

> With our incomplete knowledge of African religions, it is impossible to describe their history ... I have made no attempt in this book to deal with the historical aspects of African religions, and I am not aware of any study having been done along these lines. My approach here is chiefly descriptive and interpretative, bringing together in a comparative way those elements which are representative of traditional religions from all over Africa.[26]

Mbiti, himself, is the first to admit that, because of the religious outlook of Africans, 'their history constitutes the history of their religion'.[27] It follows that, in questioning the basis for the historical study of African religion, he is questioning the basis for the historical study of pre-colonial Africa as a whole. It is not surprising, therefore, that African historians have risen to the defence of their discipline.

49

Scholars such as Professors I. N. Kimambo and B. A. Ogot have seen in the views of Parrinder and Mbiti another form of the old accusation that Africa has no history.[28] Meanwhile, the series of conferences on the historical study of African religions, organized by the Universities of California—Los Angeles, Dar-es-Salaam, Zambia and Nairobi, and financed by the Ford Foundation of America, have striven to emphasize the possibility of the historical study of African religion and the re-integration of religious history into African historiography as a whole. This is not the place to explain and justify the methods adopted by oral historians. These are by now well accepted in professional historians' circles.[29] What is important is to indicate what can be achieved if historical questions are asked about religious ideas, beliefs, practices and institutions, and if they are seen in their right perspective as interwoven with every aspect of the past social life of Africa.

The study of African oral history has revealed a high degree of interaction between different ethnic groups. This interaction was seldom the result of great conquests or migrations, rather it was a filtering movement of small groups of people, a highly complex process of ebb and flow from every possible direction. Such a group were the Nyitumba Kimbu of Tanzania who brought with them, not only new rituals of rainmaking, but even, in all likelihood, a new concept of the supreme being.[30] In many cases an important historical personality was associated with the movement, a prestigious stranger, hunter or war-leader. Such people were often symbols of ultra-human power, and as founders of dynasties or cults became divinities themselves, like Nyikang of the Shilluk (Sudan) or Mukasa and Kintu of Buganda (Uganda).[31] Often the development of rituals in a particular area proved a source of attraction to peoples in other areas, as was the case of the life-crisis rituals of Ugweno for the Pare communities of north-eastern Tanzania.[32] At other times, the pioneering of regalia and ritual objects and their distribution by one original group provided the link between peoples. This was the case with the conus-shell disc-emblems distributed so widely in western Tanzania.[33] Such rituals and ritual objects were skilfully manipulated by political leaders in order to increase their influence and destroy opposition, and religious cults and cults of spirit mediumship frequently possessed a political role, although the ritual specialists were able in many cases to hold their own. Schoffeleers has shown how important were the shrines of the M'Bona cult in the dynastic rivalries, shifts of power, and consolidation of conquests that took place in the Zambezi valley.[34]

Historical studies have revealed the numerous ways in which religious beliefs and practices have developed over the years. Unresolved contradictions and conflicts in African religious systems may be the result of historical interaction and development, and an example of this would appear to be the apparently conflicting ideas of the supreme being among the Iramba of Tanzania.[35] At any rate, it is extremely imprudent for the scholar of religion in Africa to ignore the historical depth of the material he is studying.

To sum up this brief appraisal of African religious history, it can no longer be plausibly maintained that African religions have no history. Furthermore, the recent achievements of African historians go a long way towards offering a solution to our methodological problem. They do actually provide evidence for the diffusion of religious ideas and for cross-cultural contact on, at least, a limited basis, besides showing us how different human groups were obliged to come to terms with the same or similar religious ideas and institutions.

6 The Limited Comparative Approach

The best exponent of this method was the late Sir Edward Evans-Pritchard, a social anthropologist who was fully aware of the relationship of his discipline to that of history. His thought on the subject is contained in two lectures, The Hobhouse Memorial Trust Lecture on 'The Comparative Method in Social Anthropology' delivered in 1963 and the lecture given at Manchester University on 'Anthropology and History' in 1961.[36] Evans-Pritchard begins by conceding that comparison is one of the science's essential procedures and one of the elementary processes of human thought. He also concedes that if any general statements are to be made about social institutions they can only be made by comparison between the same types in a wide range of societies. He then takes a look at the various ways in which the classical anthropologists handled the comparative method.

McLennan used the method in order to construct a historical hypothesis which, without any historical evidence, could not be shown to be true or false. Spencer based his classifications on crude qualitative approximations bedevilled by inappropriate biological analogies, and his so-called 'congruities' were dubious, general and unhelpful. Like those of McLennan, Spencer's hypotheses were based on totally inadequate ethnographic information. Tylor's use of the comparative method is instructive only in so far as it furnishes us with some of the method's inherent problems—particularly the problem of isolating units of comparison of equivalent value. Tylor did not go beyond agreements and differences and the idea of concomitant variations was unknown to him. Breaking away from the evolutionist tradition that characterized McLennan, Spencer and Tylor, Nieboer attempted an economic classification of states rather than stages and he was followed by Hobhouse, Wheeler and Ginsberg in a similar, but much wider, study.[37] These two, later surveys benefited from a greater availability of sources, but the comparisons were on too vast a scale for their authors to exercise the necessary control over the ethnographic data. In common with most studies of this kind, their very general conclusions could, for the most part, have been foreseen. More serious still, Evans-Pritchard notes that these vast surveys can only pose questions. They cannot provide the answers and explanations for the correlations. In Evans-Pritchard's view, Radcliffe-Brown was the perfect example of a scholar who manufactured plausible explanations for apparent similarities, neglecting in the process all other material relating to the topic in question. Finally, Murdock's statistical survey covering 250 societies[38] is criticized for poor sampling, crude itemization and inadequate criteria of classification.

For Evans-Pritchard the emphasis in comparison should be placed on differences, rather than on similarities, although he admits that institutions must be similar in some respects before they can be different in others. This leads him to suggest that comparison has the best chances of success in circumstances where societies have much in common structurally, culturally and environmentally. Such intensive comparison on a limited scale was favoured by Durkheim and was proposed by Schapera and Eggan as well as by

Evans-Pritchard himself. Schapera advocates the delimitation of geographical regions in which the different human groups have strong cultural affinities, but Evans-Pritchard points out that in some geographical regions of Africa a more rigorous selection has to be made, and he thinks that such comparison is more likely to lead to historical conclusions about the factual interaction of peoples than to laws of the natural science type.

It can be seen, therefore, that the limited comparative approach, as proposed by Evans-Pritchard, is not only not opposed to the historical method; it actually presupposes it. Evans-Pritchard believed that if any generalizations were to be made that would hold good, phenomena of the same kind as the data of history—especially social history—must be used, even if only selectively and to test the conclusions reached by studies of preliterate societies. Development trends in social evolution can only be discovered if the facts of history are used, and we cannot even test the validity of our assumptions that such entities as 'society' or 'structure' exist without recourse to history. Speaking of dangerous analogies from biological science, Evans-Pritchard wrote:

> On them has been based the argument that just as we can understand the anatomy and physiology of a horse without requiring to know anything about its descent from a five-toed ancestor, so we can understand the structure of a society and the functioning of its institutions without knowing anything about its history. But a society, however defined, in no way resembles a horse, and mercifully, horses remain horses—or at least they have done so in historic times—and do not turn into elephants or pigs, whereas a society may change from one type to another, sometimes with great suddenness and violence.[39]

Terms such as 'society', 'structure' and 'function' can only be defined in relation to historical change. In the final analysis, Evans-Pritchard would have seen no difference between the historical method and his own limited comparative method, but he would (and did) stress the importance of history learning from social anthropology in the study of preliterate peoples, as well as the importance of limiting the scope of one's comparisons.

7 The Categorical Approach

To many the limited comparative approach might appear altogether too cautious and unproductive. The categorical approach is really an attempt to develop the limited comparative approach a little further. Geographical contiguity is far from being an index, let alone the only index, of historical interaction. In Africa ideas, institutions and words have often travelled very far indeed and the evidence for such a filtering process may be impossible to obtain. On the other hand, societies which are very distant from one another may be structurally, culturally and environmentally similar, even if there are no obvious historical links to explain the similarities. If such multi-dimensional similarities can be demonstrated and can be shown to outweigh the differences and variations even when these are taken carefully into consideration, we end up with just another version of the limited comparative approach in which differences serve to highlight a basic similarity.

The next question to ask is whether it is both legitimate and profitable to take these areas of comparability as categories and to point out the differences that exist between them. There can be less objection to concentrating on a wide range of differences than on a wide range of similarities, since there are more grounds for assuming that societies and institutions are different than for thinking they are the same. However, although there may be nothing objectionable in demonstrating differences between a limited number of categories, it may be objected that such a procedure does not advance our knowledge since, by definition and intention, it deals with disagreements and differences rather than with similarities and historical links. The answer of the categorizers is that the objection is a valid one and that the categories are not intended to prove or disprove relationships between them, but merely to offer the scholar elements with which to understand a given cultural situation. Although, obviously, they stand by their categories, they do not necessarily insist that their list is exhaustive, or that their categories could not, in fact, be sub-divided in the light of further evidence. The making of categories is a continuing, not a once-and-for-all task, and it is for other scholars to decide, in their areas, whether the categories as they stand are useful or not and whether or not they have to be modified.

One example of the attempt to establish categories is provided by Joseph Goetz.[40] For him the most interesting and fruitful method of studying traditional religions is to take each type of culture and make a list of all its religious elements, tracing them back to their foundations in the living experience of a particular environment. Goetz's standpoint is really socio-psychological, the study of the different forms religion takes as a result of human reactions to a particular social ecology or way of life. His conclusions are necessarily general, but (I believe) they are nonetheless helpful. For Goetz there are two basic categories: theism and deism in the light of which other elements of religion can be studied, spirits, myths and symbols, rites and cults. Although the division appears simple, in actual fact the two categories stand at either end of a spectrum into which most forms of traditional religion can be fitted.

In its pure form, theism is the experience of the supreme being as both one and many, as overwhelming, having a direct and effective influence on man in his daily life. He is the owner and conserver of all things and he punishes the abuse of his creation by man. His presence is felt to be close, even though it takes no tangible form and he reveals himself in moral relationships and in good or bad use of material things by man. Goetz sees this kind of belief as typifying the religions of unspecified hunter-gatherers and shifting cultivators, as well as of pastoralists—both ecological types of passivity to a vast and scantily peopled environment.

At the other end of the spectrum lies deism, a concept of God without any religious reality—a supreme being acknowledged but not seen to play an explicit role in the life of man or even in his community rituals. However deism is usually characterized by a highly developed theology and a concept of world order that places the supreme being outside man's world. Deism is most commonly found among settled cultivators, groups which are more active in modifying their environment, and whose social and political structures are stronger and more enduring, giving rise to hierarchies of ancestral and territorial spirits. Goetz is far from being inflexible about these categories, and easily admits that, for example, a society of settled cultivators can also possess a particular specialization in hunting, in which case, the categories may apply to different situations within the same culture.

Mary Douglas bases her categories on criteria that are more sociological.[41] For her, the different forms of religious belief and practice are products of definable social experience. Her scheme is at once subtle and complex, and although she describes four basic categories which result from combinations of varying strengths of group experience and personal networks, each of these divisions is susceptible of variation from zero, where social relationships possess a minimum of structure, to an upper limit in which the characteristics of the category in question are fully developed. Mary Douglas does not label her categories, but her comprehensive picture of theology, morality, and symbolism in each section results in a schema which harmonizes well with that of Goetz. I have ventured to call the categories: strong theism, integrated or relative theism, deistic dualism and secularism—bearing in mind that these names refer only to the theological aspect of thought systems.[42]

Both Goetz and Douglas base their categories upon the study of a certain number of existing societies and they assume that other societies could also be assimilated to the same categories. However, they do not indulge in a wholesale classification and have no sympathy with such an exercise. The categories are basically models designed to help a scholar understand any given situation, and not a substitute for the serious study of each society in its own right. We are still left, therefore, with the problem of whether we can in any way bridge the gap that yawns between the various categories.

8 The Thematic Approach

One way of bridging the gap is to select a rather general theme and to study it in the different contexts, noting its relative position and function, and its various meanings and applications. This may not be comparison, strictly speaking, but it does increase our knowledge by revealing the dimensions of the theme in question. This is what Canon Harry Sawyerr of Fourah Bay College has done for the concept of God in three major West African Societies.[43] Although, like many other African writers on Traditional Religion, he is a theologian rather than an anthropologist, Sawyerr takes an anthropological view. He fully understands that the supreme being in the societies he studies is not a philosophical concept, but rather an experience approached symbolically through different aspects of man's life in the world. Consequently, he studies it in the language, literature, social life and institutions of each ethnic group, making copious use of the work of previous scholars in the field.

The three societies studied by Sawyerr are the Akan of Ghana, the Mende of Sierra Leone and the Yoruba of Nigeria. All three combine the concept of a supreme being with an emphasis on divinities and ancestral spirits. Sawyerr describes the relative importance of two guiding images of the supreme being that are present in each of the cases. The first image derives from the experience of birth or descent, according to which the supreme being is pictured as an ancestor, the first and greatest ancestor of all men. The second image is based on man's experience of modifying his natural environment, working with tools and developing crafts. According to this image, the supreme being is the creator and master-craftsman. However, in all of the societies under study the experience of the sacred or the numinous is at once a unity and a diversity and the cult of the supreme being is effectively displaced by that of divinities in the sphere of nature and craftsmanship, and by that of ancestral spirits in the sphere of the transmission of life through birth and descent. Sawyerr goes on to study, among other things, the related notion of re-incarnation and notes the relative importance of the concept among the Akan and the Yoruba, and its relative unimportance among the Mende.

Within his self-imposed limitations—even because of them —Sawyerr achieves a great deal in this thematic study. We need many more examples of this type of study and fewer of the pan-African or sub-Saharan studies which we have been getting in recent years. Sawyerr, however, did not take these three West African peoples as examples of a particular category or categories, although it turns out that they have a great deal in common both in the structure of their beliefs and in their physical and social environments. The next step to take is to carry out a similar thematic enquiry among different categories or representatives of different categories such as those proposed in the last section of this chapter.

9 Multi-dimensional Approaches

If progress is to be made in the comparative study of African religions, then the strengths of all the approaches outlined in the last four sections of this chapter must be combined. Categories should be established on the basis of structural, cultural and environmental similarity and, where this is available, on evidence of historic interaction or contact. These categories should then become the starting-point for thematic studies. Very little work of this kind has been done, and what follows is a very recent attempt to sketch out such a study.[44] More work must be done on it to correct it and fill it out. It remains very much of a blueprint.

The aim was to examine the prayer literature of the living African tradition as recorded by ethnographers and students of oral literature. 152 texts were studied in the context of the religious cultures from which they came. In the light of this study and of the findings of both Goetz and Douglas, six categories were established. These categories reflected different 'prayer models' that combined the variables: supreme being/divinities and mediators, and experiential/ formal prayer. Fifteen themes were then selected from the texts. Some of these related directly to the variables in the models, but others reflected the raw material of prayer, the life-situation of the worshipper or his declared purpose in praying. Finally, a very interesting group of themes emerged from the prayer-dynamic itself, themes such as the trans- mission of life, the concepts of memorial and judgement and so forth. These themes were then examined in the different contexts represented by the categories already established. In a few cases the themes did not appear at all, but to the majority of the categories the themes were relevant, although they received very varied treatment. The study consisted in noting the differences of approach in each category to the same or similar themes.

The future of the comparative study of African religions appears to lie with the limited, rather than the generalizing, approaches. Historical research will play an increasingly im- portant role, as will the kind of thematic and categorical approaches which we have described. In the chapters that follow examples of these methods will be given in greater detail in order to demonstrate the sort of thing that can be achieved by them.

Notes

1. Abbott, Walter, A., 1966, *The Documents of Vatican II*, London, p. 662, fn. 9.

2. Neill, Stephen, 1970, *Christian Faith and Other Faiths*, Oxford, p. 129.

3. Forde, D., and Jones, G. I., 1950, *The Ibo and Ibibio-speaking People of South Eastern Nigeria*, IAI, London, p. 5.

4. Idowu, E. Bolaji, 1973, *African Traditional Religion, A Definition*, London, p. 106.

5. Barrett, David, B., 1968, *Schism and Renewal in Africa*, Nairobi, p. 45.

6. Parrinder, Geoffrey, 1969, *Religion in Africa*, Harmondsworth, p. 17.

7. Parrinder, Geoffrey, 1954, *African Traditional Religion*, London, p. 11.

8. Parrinder, Geoffrey, 1969, *Religion in Africa*, Harmondsworth, p. 9.

9. Parrinder, 1954 and 1969.

10. Cf. Dammann, E., 1962, *Die Religionen Afrikas*, Stuttgart.

11. Frazer, James G., 1922, *The Golden Bough*, (abridgement in one volume), London.

12. Abraham, W. E., 1962, *The Mind of Africa*, London, p. 46.

13. Mbiti, John S., 1969, *African Religions and Philosophy*, London, p. 1.

14. Mbiti, *ibid.*, p. 1.

15. Taylor, John V., 1963, *The Primal Vision*, London, p. 27.

16. Idowu, E. Bolaji, 1973, *African Traditional Religion, A Definition*, London, p. 103.

17. Idowu, *ibid.*, p. 103.

18. Taylor, 1963, p. 27.

19. Mbiti, 1969, pp. 1-2.

20. Abraham, 1962, p. 46.

21. Mbiti, 1969, p. 23.

22. Parrinder, 1969, p. 9.

23. Ranger, T. O., and Kimambo, I. N., 1972, *The Historical Study of African Religion*, London, p. 2.

24. Mbiti, 1969, p. 4.

25. Mbiti, 1969, p. 23.

26. Mbiti, 1969, p. 5.

27. Mbiti, 1969, p. 5.

28. Ranger and Kimambo, 1972, p. 3.

29. Cf. Ranger and Kimambo, 1972, *passim*.

30. Shorter, Aylward, 1974, 'The Historical Diffusion of Sun-Symbolism in East African Religious Thought', Paper read to Third Conference on the Historical Study of African Religion, Limuru, Kenya.

31. Cf. Nsimbi, Michael, 1974, 'Kiganda Traditional Religion', Paper read to the meeting of the Vatican Secretariat for Non-Christians, Gaba, Uganda.

32. Kimambo, I. N., 1969, *A Political History of the Pare of Tanzania*, Nairobi, pp. 47-64.

33. Shorter, Aylward, 1972, *Chiefship in Western Tanzania*, Oxford, pp. 180-188, and 242 ff.

34. Ranger and Kimambo, 1972, pp. 73-94.

35. Pender-Cudlip, Patrick, 1974, 'God and the Sun: Some Notes on Iramba Religious History', Paper presented to the Third Conference on the Historical Study of African Religion, Limuru, Kenya.

36. Evans-Pritchard, E. E. Y., 1962, *Essays in Social Anthropology*, London, pp. 46-65, and 1965, *The Position of Women in Primitive Societies and Other Essays in Social Anthropology*, London, pp. 13-36.

37. Hobhouse, L. T., Wheeler, G. C., Ginsberg, M., 1919, *The Material Culture and Social Institutions of the Simpler Peoples, An Essay in Correlation*, New York.

38. Murdock, G. P., 1949, *Social Structure*, New York.

39. Evans-Pritchard, 1962, p. 55.

40. Bergounioux, F. M., and Goetz, J., 1965, *Prehistoric and Primitive Religions*, London.

41. Douglas, Mary, 1970, *Natural Symbols*, London.

42. Shorter, Aylward, 1974, *Prayer in the Religious Traditions of Africa*, Nairobi, p. 8.

43. Sawyerr, Harry, 1970, *God, Ancestor or Creator?*, London.

44. Shorter, 1974.

Chapter IV

God and the Sun in the Religious Thought of East Africa[1]—Historical Case Study

1 Introduction

The purpose of this chapter is to demonstrate what can be achieved through the application of the historical approach to the comparative study of African religions. We shall be dealing with the religions of a wide range of societies in East Africa, particularly those of western Tanzania. However, one among all these societies provides us with an opening or starting-point for a hypothesis which can be applied to the others. This is the Kimbu people, a Bantu-speaking group who inhabit an area of west central Tanzania between latitudes 5° and 8° south and longitudes 32° and 35° east. Their country is bounded and crossed by several large rivers, the Rungwa, Njombe, Nkululu and Lupa, while in the southwest their territory follows the eastern shore of Lake Rukwa. Kimbu country lies at an altitude of between 3,500 feet and 7,000 feet above sea-level, and it contains many high hills with red granite outcrops. The country is evenly and densely wooded with trees of nectar-producing varieties. Its surface area is some 20,000 square miles and it is sparsely inhabited by about 50,000 people concentrated in some eighty isolated villages, on or near the three main roads that cross the country.

The Kimbu are hunter-gatherers and shifting maize cultivators. They are especially keen honey collectors. Their social and political structure is complex, there being thirty-eight chiefdoms, grouped in five associations. The core of each association is an original founder dynasty, but settler dynasties have been admitted at various periods. The Kimbu have thirteen dispersed patri-clans, and descent is patrilineal except where succession to the chiefly office is concerned. In this case the rule of descent is matrilineal. Kimbu religion reflects the two theatres of their life, the forest and village-

61

clearing. The forest is thought to be the abode of largely malevolent nature spirits, while the village is the home of benevolent lineage spirits, the spirits of those buried there. The territorial spirits which are the lineage spirits of chiefly families are ambivalent, sharing both in the malevolence and power of the spirits of the forest where their graves are situated and in the creative and life-giving attributes of the supreme being himself. Kimbu chiefs are divine rulers, being in themselves pledges of divine favour for their people.

Kimbu history begins before the end of the 17th century with the arrival from the north-east of the Nyisamba who occupied the Kimbu heartland and who founded the largest association of chiefdoms. In the early 18th century they were joined by the Nyitumba who came from the eastern Tanzanian hinterland and who were already in touch with the coast for the purposes of trade. Not only was the arrival of the Nyitumba accompanied by the introduction of new crops and by an impetus given to iron-working, but the newcomers also introduced the conus-shell disc-emblem, made from the cone shaped shells found on the East African coast. The conus-shell disc-emblem is symbolically linked in Kimbu thought with the sun and the sky, and the evidence points to the introduction of a new emphasis in Kimbu thought as a result of the coming of the Nyitumba. Furthermore, the Kimbu as a whole became, in their turn, the most active group engaged in spreading the conus-shell regalia and symbolism, and the evidence suggests that the distribution of conus-shells over the whole area of western Tanzania coincided with a similar change of emphasis in religious thought and symbolism.[2]

2 Etymological Indications

It is a fact that a large number of East African peoples link the sun symbolically with the supreme being. Harjula has listed eight Tanzanian and Kenyan peoples who do so, the Kuria, Mbugwe, Sonjo, Pare, Issanzu, Iramba, Gogo and Pimbwe, besides the Tanzanian Meru and Chagga who were the special object of his study.[3] His list was not intended to be exhaustive and, indeed, there are a great many more: the Turu or Rimi ('People of the Sun')[4] in Central Tanzania, the Kimbu of south-western Tanzania, the peoples of Greater Unyamwezi and Usukuma and the Iraqw in central Tanzania, the Haya of the north-west, the Kuria of northern Tanzania, the Ganda, Ankole, Kiga and Nyoro of southern and western Uganda, as well as the southern Nilotic peoples and the Kalenjin—in particular, the Marakwet—of western Kenya. This symbolic link may take various semantic forms. All over the world peoples of different cultures have likened the supreme being to the sun in the sky through the use of simile or metaphor. We find this practice, for example, quite frequently in the Old Testament.[5] In such cases we may speak of the 'sun-attribute' of the supreme being. It should be made clear, however, from the start, that in East Africa we are dealing with something more than a sun-attribute. In many cases, the semantic linkage between supreme being and sun takes the form of a single word being used for both, although—as Harjula easily demonstrates—there is no question of a failure to distinguish between the two. In quite a number of cases, however, the supreme being is given a 'sun-name', distinct from the ordinary word used for the sun in the sky, but it is known to refer to the supreme being in his sun aspect. The following table gives the terminology for most of the peoples mentioned:

Name of the People	Sun-Name of Supreme Being	Word for sun when this is different from Sun-Name
Marakwet, Nandi	*Asis*	
Gusii	*Erioba*	
Mbugwe	*Djua*	
Sonjo	*Riob*	
Pare	*Izuva*	
Issanzu	*Dyiova*	
Iramba	*Nzua*	
Gogo	*Inzua*	
Meru	*Iruva*	
Chagga	*Iruva (Rua)*	
Turu (Rimi)	*Yuva*	
Pimbwe (Mpimbwe)	*Ilyuba*	*limi*
Kimbu	*Ilyuva*	*ilyunsi*
Nyamwezi, Sukuma	*Lyoba, Lyuba, Zyoba, Kazyoba*	*limi*

Name of the People	Sun-Name of Supreme Being	Word for sun when this is different from Sun-Name
Haya	*Kazooba*	*eizooba*
Ganda	*Kazooba*	*enjuba*
Ankole, Kiga, Nyoro	*Kazooba*	*eizooba*

Looking at the table it can be seen at a glance that most of the peoples employ a single word for the sun in the sky and for the supreme being in his sun aspect. However, there are nine groups which make a terminological distinction between them. Of these the Ugandan peoples and the closely related Haya of north-western Tanzania use terms which are etymologically related, both word for sun and sun-name being derived from the common Bantu root, *-uba -ooba*. It is only the peoples of western Tanzania who use terms with differing derivations. For both the Kimbu and the Nyamwezi / Sukuma, the word for sun (*ilyunsi* and *limi* respectively) means also sunlight, daylight, day, day-time, but the Ugandan peoples have another word for this meaning. In the case of the Kimbu the word *ilyunsi* is related to the term for dry season, *cunsi*, and this is paralleled in Swahili, the *lingua franca* of East Africa, in which *anga*, light or sunshine, is related to *kiangazi*, dry season, or season when the sunshine is strongest. The Nyamwezi, however, use the word *kipwa* for dry season, a term which refers to the cutting of grass, and not to sunshine.[6] We are further faced with an interesting correlation. The peoples who distinguish in this way between sun and sun-name, the peoples of western Tanzania, are the very same peoples who traditionally employ conus-shell regalia.

Linguistic history throws considerable light on the problem. According to Ehret, the semantic linkage of sun and supreme being was a characteristic of the Rift Southern Cushitic languages which spread over western and central Kenya and into northern and central Tanzania during the last millennium B.C.[7] Through loan words and loan translations, it seems likely that religious ideas expressed in the Southern Cushitic languages influenced both the Southern Nilotic languages and the languages of the Bantu peoples about 2,000 years ago and 1,000 years ago respectively. The use of a single word for both supreme being and sun, of the root, -ova, -oba, -ooba, -uva, -uba, -ua, is therefore probably a practice of considerable antiquity. This is corroborated by the Kimbu informant who told me in 1966 that *Ilyuva*, the present sun-name for the supreme being, was, in the past, the word used for the sun itself. Although, when making oaths and calling the supreme being to witness the truth of what they say, the Kimbu point to the sun in the sky and say: '*Ilyuva* is there!' (*Ilyuva alili*), or '*Ilyuva* has seen it' (*Ilyuva liwine*), no Kimbu today would think of referring to the sun itself as *Ilyuva*. On the contrary, people say: 'The sun is hot' (*lixal'ilyunsi*) or they speak about the sun (*ilyunsi*) sweetening or burning the earth, according to context. The same is true for the Nyamwezi peoples, and their use of *limi* (sun). In 1961, Schönenberger expressed the opinion that the Nyamwezi names for the supreme being in his aspect of creator, *Matunda*, *Msumbi* and *Kube* were an older usage than the sun-names *Lyuba*, *Zyoba*, and *Kazyoba*.[8] If this opinion is correct, it may refer to pre-Cushitic times, or it may more plausibly refer to the fact that ritual developments and elaborations of the supreme being/sun linkage occurred at a later date than the introduction of the loan translation itself.

A hypothesis which emerges from the linguistic evidence is that the Kimbu and Nyamwezi/Sukuma peoples, in common with the Bantu peoples of western Uganda, possessed a single term for sun and sun-name. However, at a certain point in time the sun-name received a new emphasis or prominence in the religious thought of these Tanzanian peoples, so much so that the term became exclusively reserved for the sun-name, and it was necessary to extend the meaning of another word, the word for light or sunshine, to include that of the sun in the sky. At the present time this word for sunshine now refers to the heavenly body itself and not just the light emanating from it. If this is so, and in the light of the fact that these western Tanzanian peoples are the very ones who accepted the conus-shell regalia from the east coast, we may consider the further hypothesis that this change of theological emphasis coincided with the arrival of the conus-shells.

3 Evidence for a Re-structuring of Kimbu Religious Thought

The main support for our hypothesis comes from the relative importance of different kinds of Kimbu regalia at different periods of history. Besides the conus-shell disc-emblem which has been given such importance in modern times, there is an older item of Kimbu regalia, unknown to the Nyamwezi peoples, called *imbutu*, or ghost-horn.[9] This instrument is a long, curved, side-blown horn made of wood. It is very often about five feet in length, though it is sometimes smaller. It is made in several pieces with the joints covered by sleeves of black cow-hide. The wood is elaborately carved with geometrical designs and there is usually a knob at the top in the form of a human head. The ghost-horn is still an object of great veneration among the Kimbu.

The narratives which describe the coming of the Nyitumba Kimbu, together with their neighbours, the Bungu people, of the Rukwa plain, refer to the conus-shells which they brought with them and with which their chiefs were invested. The first certain mention of conus-shells among the Nyisamba Kimbu who were the first arrivals in the area dates to the second half of the 18th century, after the arrival of the Nyitumba. At this time the senior Nyisamba chief granted the right to wear conus-shell emblems to one Kawenga, founder of the Rukwa chiefdom of Manda. Kawenga, however, was refused the right to have a ghost-horn. In an exactly parallel situation, the Nyitumba chief of Kipembawe at about the same date made a grant of regalia to the Mya chiefdom of Ilundu. In this case, the ghost-horn was granted, but the right to wear the conus-shell was withheld. These differing attitudes to the regalia are very revealing, since they show that soon after the coming of the Nyitumba the Nyisamba esteemed the ghost-horn more than the conus-shell. By the time of my fieldwork in the 1960s, the Nyisamba attitude had become that of the Nyitumba.

Not only was it much easier to see and to photograph ghost-horns, in contrast to the great secrecy which surrounded the conus-shell emblems among the Nyisamba, but I was told by the senior Nyisamba chief that the conus-shell was 'the most important thing in the chiefdom', so sacred that it was impossible for a stranger to view it.

66

We must now consider the religious symbolism that surrounds the two items of regalia. The ghost-horn is clearly associated with the earth or country (*nsi*), and it is commonly called 'honour of the earth' (*isima yaansi*) or just simply 'earth' (*nsi*). The horn is made of red *Pterocarpus* wood which resembles the colour of earth, and its name *imbutu*, although it means literally 'white thing', refers not to its colour but to its sacred character. The ghost-horn is the special emblem of the Kimbu chief and his family who are also identified with earth and country. When a chief died at the hands of an enemy, it was said: 'The earth is dead.' The chief was forbidden to handle earth or to hoe the earth like other people, and when he died he was buried in the earth in a sitting, life-like posture, unlike commoners whose corpses were probably, formerly left in the bush. Marrying a woman of the matrilineal, chiefly dynasty was called 'planting the earth', in other words, making the country fruitful by raising up seed to the chief's family. The chief himself was often called 'the one of the country' (*umunyaansi*) and his relatives were called 'son of the country', 'nephew of the country', 'sister of the country' and so on, according to their relationship. The ghost-horn was only blown for the installation of a new chief, on the return of a chief to his country after a journey, when sacrifice was offered to the ancestors of the chief at their graves in the forest, and finally, when a runaway female slave was found in the forest and added to the chief's harem. On this last occasion it was said: 'The earth has brought her.' Many ghost-horns today have a solar symbol carved on them, the coil design, concentric circles, or disc with projecting rays, but this may be a modern practice and there is certainly no idea of the ghost-horn coming from *Ilyuva*, like the conus-shell emblem.

The earth in Kimbu thought was a female symbol, and it was women who traditionally planted seeds in the earth, made pottery and earthenware and carried out earth and mud plastering when building was going on. Because of his association with the earth, the chief was symbolically female also and at his installation had his hair plaited like that of a woman. Women, too, played the principal roles in the ritual, the songs and the dances. The myth charter of the Nyitumba celebrates the coming of a stranger from eastern

Tanzania to marry a woman of the chiefly dynasty and the Nyisamba myth charter traces the original dynasty back to a foundress, a woman called Isamba.

Besides *Ilyuva*, the Kimbu have another name for the supreme being, *Matunda*. This name comes from an ancient word *-tunda* meaning to mould or make pottery and refers to the supreme being in his aspect of creator. The work of the creator is analogous to that of a woman moulding pottery, and the hills on which the chief's ancestors are buried are associated with *Matunda* and the above. In fact, the very word for hill or mountain is *ikitunda* 'the thing of the creator'. The word for 'the above', *igulu*, also features prominently in the names given to hills,[10] and to chiefdoms which very often take their name from the hills which are their ritual centres. Although *Ilyuva* features in popular oaths, the name hardly appears in religious song and poetry. Here it is nearly always *Matunda*. Neither name appears in the prayer formulas used during sacrifice. On these occasions attention is focused on the territorial spirits or guardians of the earth, the deceased chiefs. The suggestion is that this is the older cosmic picture of the Kimbu, and that in this picture they do not raise their eyes very far from the earth which is, indeed, their central preoccupation. It is to the hills, rather than to the heavens that they turn, and although—as we shall see—*igulu* re-appears in some of the song texts associated with *Ilyuva* and the conus-shell, we find that clouds are more important than hills in the new cosmic picture. More common than *igulu* today is *xwilunde*, 'the place of the clouds'.[11]

The conus-shell disc-emblem which is worn on the chief's forehead is called by the Kimbu *impaji*, and the most important evidence for its association with *Ilyuva* is provided by the texts of songs sung at the installation of the chief, by throne-names and praise-names used by chiefs and by certain expressions which are used in connection with the chief. All of these show that the supreme being in his sun aspect is at the centre of a whole sky cosmology, symbolized by the chief and his *impaji*. A portion of one of the installation songs reads as follows:

Ee 'mwaana 'musyomi	O, Son of the stranger
nafumile xutali	I come from far
xwigulu nanuxo	There, up in the heavens

xwafumil'impaji	The conus-shell came forth
n'imixowa iyo	And the conus-shell straps
xwalemil'impungu	Even the eagle was left behind
alindelembe[12]	When I soared aloft.

Here we are in another world altogether, a world of height, distance, heavens, and high-flying birds like the eagle. Chief and conus-shell are mystically united and both appear in the heavens. The chief is the charismatic stranger from afar. When a chief dies his death is euphemistically referred to by the phrase: 'It (the sun) has clouded over' (*ilunde lyatelaga*). Among the throne-names and praise-names one finds not only the ubiquitous *Mpaji* itself, but also *Kifumigulu*, 'thing which came from the heavens', *Mpela Malunde* and *Kapela Malunde*, 'giver of clouds', and *Mukowa*, 'strap with which the conus-shell is tied on'. The significance of the name 'giver of clouds' is that it is the chief's task to bring rain-clouds, and it is known that the Nyitumba brought with them new rituals of rain-making which involved the use of round, white stones, symbolic of the sun and other astral bodies. They also brought with them new seeds and may have introduced the use of iron hoes. Consequently their coming coincided with a new emphasis on agriculture in Kimbu history, as opposed to hunting and gathering, and also with a greater dependence on regular rainfall.

If one asks a Kimbu: 'Where do the conus-shells come from?' one can receive an answer at any one of three levels:

They come from the coast or a trader from the coast	Physical provenance
They come from another chiefdom	Origin of the right to regalia
They come from *Ilyuva*	Symbolic origin

The connection, therefore, of the conus-shell with *Ilyuva* is quite explicit. Moreover, coming from the east, the place of the rising sun, the Nyitumba were identified with their own sun symbolism. Those who settled in Kiwele in central Ukimbu were known as *Nyalyuva*, the people of *Ilyuva*, and they, together with the Igulwibi Kimbu who had settled for a time in Iramba before migrating back to Ukimbu use a clan-name and greeting meaning 'the fierce one', *Nyankali*. There is not only a clan-name in Iramba today which is similar, *Anankali*, but the name 'Fierce One', *Munankali* is there regularly applied to *Nzua*, the supreme being in his sun-aspect.

The Iramba case is interesting. According to Pender-Cudlip, the older names for the creator, *Tyunda Mulungu*, have been supplanted to such an extent by the sun-name, *Nzua*, that the relationship of the two aspects has not even been worked out.[13] However, it would seem that no need arose in Iramba to coin a new word for the sun in the sky. The word *nzua* continues to be used for both, although another word *lyua* sometimes appears in the meaning of 'luck', an aspect of the supreme being and his providence covered for the Kimbu by the single word *Ilyuva*.

In all the cultures of East Africa that employ a sun-name for the supreme being, the two attributes of the sun in the sky, giving life, and destroying it are applied to him. The sun sweetens the earth, quickens and gives life to crops. On the other hand, it burns fiercely, drying up the earth and withering thirsty plants. In the same way the supreme being is the master of mankind and arbiter of his actions. He gives life to man and punishes his evil deeds. His is the power of life and death. For the Kimbu, *Ilyuva* is life-giver and first ancestor, rather than creator, and this character is strengthened by his symbolic maleness. The supreme being in his sun aspect is essentially male and the Iramba neighbours of the Kimbu have a picturesque way of describing the sun's daily progress from the east until it sinks into the earth in the west. They say that the sun rises from his 'men's quarters' (*numba ya kigosha*), travels all day and arrives at his 'wife's quarters' (*numba ya kikima*) in the evening.[14] For the Kimbu, as for many other East African peoples, the male is the active principle in procreation, the source of life, and it is significant that a woman on the marriage bed is supposed to face east. In the Kimbu birth rites, the male child is brought out of the house at sunrise, while the female child is brought out at sunset.

The idea of the supreme being as life-giver, rather than creator, is the key idea of the sky-centred cosmology and it finds its way into the myths and oral literature of the Kimbu. A good example is provided by an etiological story purporting to explain the origin of rats and their relationship to mankind.[15] The story is designed to show that rats are the real masters of the world and that all the crops that man plants, reaps and threshes are ultimately for the benefit of the rats who raid his food-store. Man works and the rats profit by man's sweat. The reason that rats are in this privileged situation is that the supreme being has sold mankind into slavery to the rats as a result of a debt. It is not necessary to go into all the details of this highly original story. What is important for our present purposes is the picture which the story gives of the origin of mankind. At the beginning, we are told, men were living with their chief in 'the above' beyond the clouds. The chief is called *Nkuva* ('drum-beater'), a circumlocution for *Ilyuva*, since this is a somewhat cynical and disrespectful story. We give here the first part of the story.

In the past the king of the world was *Ikwija*, the rat. Today we call him 'rat' (*imbeva*), but in those far off days he was called *Ikwija* and he had many children. We human beings were not here on earth. We were up there in heaven where *Nkuva* lived. We lived there, and everything was there. Here on earth *Ikwija* had a drum which sounded very musical. When *Nkuva* let his rain fall from heaven in heavy torrents, accompanied by lightning, *Ikwija* sounded his drum. The sound of the drum was heard everywhere on earth and his people could hear it, and even in heaven where *Nkuva* lived with his people it could be heard. 'Ah', said *Nkuva*, 'my people, this thing which roars down there when we look down from above produces a very loud sound. If we had this drum up here it would be very convenient.' His people replied, 'Ah, Master, it would be very nice to have it here.' 'But' (continued *Nkuva*) 'there is no way of reaching him (*Ikwija*) and he hides the drum. When I shine on him I can see him. The light of my fire-brand reaches the earth and I can see him drumming. But they are very clever and hide it.'

The rain continued until the end of the wet season and *Ikwija*'s drum could still be heard. When it sounded it could be heard everywhere—even as far as Chunya town.[16] That was the drum of *Ikwija*, the king of the earth. *Nkuva* only brought rain here on earth. We, his people, were there in heaven with him. All the cows were there, all the goats and everything, including food, was there in heaven. Here on earth lived *Ikwija* and his children by themselves. Whenever *Ikwija* was pleased—even during the dry season—he played his drum. The sound of the drum was heard all over the earth, and even those living as far away as Kipembawe recognized the drum of *Ikwija*.[17] *Nkuva*, up there in heaven, was not pleased at all. 'Ah' (he said) 'the person who lives down below there, the place we see when we are looking down, has a drum with a very nice sound, but the distance between us is too great.' His people replied, 'Our Master, if you were the owner of that drum it would be a good thing.'

Nkuva, thereupon, called a meeting to find out what his people thought about *Ikwija*'s drum. 'My people,' *Nkuva* began, 'if I go and steal *Ikwija*'s drum, what can happen? Do you think he will come up here, if I take his drum?' 'Master,' said his people, 'we do not know. It is for yourself to decide.' (*Nkuva* went on), 'When I light my firebrand, its light reaches the earth and I see *Ikwija* walking with his small legs. If I steal his drum what can happen?' They replied, 'It is in your power to do as you please. We think that if the drum is brought here, heaven will be a nice place to live in.' (*Nkuva* concluded), 'Tomorrow I shall try and pour down some rain.'

Next day he shook the clouds and rain poured down in heavy torrents *pwa-pwa-pwa*. When he saw the rain, *Ikwija* was happy. He took his drum and started playing it. Its sound was heard everywhere, as far away as Ngwala and Ubungu.[18] The drum of *Ikwija* was known everywhere, but he lived with his own children by themselves. There were no men. Then said *Nkuva*, 'Now I shall pluck up courage and go and steal the drum. It interests me very much.' His people said, 'If you have the courage, go and take it.' (*Nkuva* replied), 'He is very clever and his children too are very clever. After drumming, they hide it.' The people said, 'One day he will be late. He will leave it in the sun, and because your eyes reach the earth, you will be able to get it. We, your people, our eyes do not reach the earth but your eyes do reach it.' 'Yes,' said *Nkuva*, 'when I look down I even see the drummer himself. He is very small but the drum has a good rhythm.' The people finally urged him, 'Go and steal it. Where will he get through to reach us here?' One day *Ikwija* put his drum in the sun and went away. *Nkuva* immediately shook the clouds and rain started falling. When he opened his eyes he saw the drum and took it up to heaven. *Ikwija* came to the place where he had left his drum and found it was not there. 'Children,' *Ikwija* asked, 'there is no drum. It was here in the sun. Who has taken it?' 'We don't know,' they said. 'Ah-ah-ah, look for it.' So they started searching everywhere for the drum, but all in vain.

Up there *Nkuva* stirred the clouds and rain started falling. When he opened his eyes and saw them looking for the drum, he beat it, grrrrrrr! 'Ah-ah-ah,' exclaimed *Ikwija*, 'the drum is being beaten in heaven. He has stolen my drum! Ka! Ee! They have killed me, my sons. The man who opens his eyes and sends light down here— *Nkuva*. It is he who has taken my drum.' He became very sad indeed and complained to his children gathered around him. Meanwhile *Nkuva* was happy playing the drum while rain fell. He beat it grrrr-grrrr, kalalala-kalalala. The sound of the drum was now twice as loud, and *Nkuva*'s people praised their king saying, 'You see now how perfect it is, when the rain is falling and the drum is sounding....'[19]

In this charming story the supreme being is pictured as a chief, living with his people above the clouds. He shakes the clouds to make rain and flashes his eye for lightning. His firebrand, the sun, also scans the earth below. Neither he nor his people seem to know very much about the earth or its inhabitants, the rats, but the chief covets the rats' thunder-drum and his people connive in its capture. The story goes on to relate how the spider spins a web between earth and heaven, how *Ikwija*, the King of rats, climbed the web and gnawed his way through heaven's thick outer crust, to confront *Nkuva* with the theft. A bargain is struck and mankind is sold into slavery on account of the drum. In this way of thinking, mankind takes its origin from the sky, not the earth, and heaven—where men, houses, goats and cattle are ready-made—provides a kind of perfect, Platonic form of earthly society.

In his account of the southern Nyamwezi (of the so-called 'Kimbu Chiefdoms') Blohm records two traditions of origin.[20] In one of them the Creator, called *Limatunda*, is responsible for bringing the whole world into existence. All comes from him and he is the proprietor of everything. In the second tradition, *Lyuba*, the sun, is presented as the first and most important creature who has brought mankind into existence. It looks very much as if the two cosmologies have been married in this second version, and that an ill-advised attempt has been made to reconcile two views of the supreme being, *Limatunda*, Creator and *Lyuba*, Life-Giver. The Nyamwezi certainly apply both names to the supreme being, and the problem of placing both in a single story of origin probably only occurred to them in response to European questioning.

I never came across any Kimbu attempt to reconcile *Matunda* and *Ilyuva* in this way, though there is one important royal myth which borrows symbolism both from earth-centred and sky-centred cosmologies. This is the myth of Ipupi. This myth contrasts with other myths which are either earth-centred or sky-centred. In the former, the hills are presented as the judgement seats of chiefs. From their summits their voices can be heard, and their enemies are thrown down to their deaths. Chiefs are depicted as wanting to move the hills from one place to another, but find that the task is too great for them. After the coming of the Bungu who accompanied the Nyitumba and who set up a chiefdom to the south of the Kimbu, we find a second series of myths which describe the futile efforts of Bungu chiefs to scale the heavens by means of platforms erected on the hills. In particular, they are said to have tried to snatch the moon from the sky—without success, and their conus-shell disc-emblem is likened to a fish vertebra. All of this was a calculated insult to the Bungu fishermen of Lake Rukwa, but the implication presumably was that the Kimbu chiefs, whose conus-shell symbolized the sun, were more successful in scaling the heavens and dispensing the sources of life and prosperity than their Bungu counterparts.

The myth of Ipupi has already been published and analysed and we need only summarize it here.[21] This myth concerns the founder Nyisamba chiefdom which is called Wikangulu. Ipupi was the third of the rulers of Wikangulu, and his praise name *Chogopya Valavi*, means 'Terror of those who wake'. His village was built on the slopes of a high hill called Nyalanga, the summit of which was crowned by a tall, finger-like rock. Not only did Ipupi, according to the story, call his junior chiefs (with the aid of a magic gourd-bow) and dispense his judgements from the top of the hill—a variation on other earth-centred myths—but he was also found mysteriously seated at sunrise on top of the rock-pinnacle, and his bearded, shining face inspired terror in all who beheld him at dawn. At the end of his life, so the story relates, Ipupi descended living into the earth, but significantly this took place at sunset, when the sun also sinks into the earth. Ipupi enjoyed power of life and death over his 'children'. Moreover, like *Nkuva* in the other story quoted, Ipupi handed recalcitrant subjects over to rats for punishment which, like the rats of the earlier story, devoured the crops cultivated by man. Ipupi also possessed an instant-aneous control over rain and sunshine. Yet, even in this story in which such phenomenal celestial powers are attrib-uted to a chief, human finiteness is celebrated by the descent of Ipupi into the earth and by the breaking and tumbling down of his rock-pinnacle after his disappearance. This downward movement is discernible in all the chiefly myths and the theme of the Ipupi story is no different. Its interest, however, is that, in the versions which are told today, celestial details are included in order to enhance Ipupi's stature as the 'great chief in the country of Wikangulu' and 'Our Master'.[22]

4 An Enlargement of Theological Scale

Professor Monica Wilson has discussed the idea that, with a change in the scale of human relationships, goes a change in religious awareness and theological understanding.[23] A development often occurs in the idea of God who becomes less shadowy and more personal. Even the conception of life itself changes; sin is less closely linked to misfortune and intrinsic quality is thought of as relatively separate from particular acts. The idea of suffering as creative also makes an appearance. The radical change is not simply the addition of an idea of God or a change in the spatial symbols which men use when speaking of him. It is a step in the direction of monotheism, with the supreme being as the sole author of life.

I would submit that something of the sort occurred among the Kimbu of Tanzania during the 18th century. Under the influence of the Nyitumba travellers, their horizons were extended and the scale of their social relationships was enlarged. The idea of the supreme being received a new, strong emphasis and the spatial symbols used regarding him were changed into more sublime, celestial ones. The sun-symbolism of the supreme being, in particular, possessed a more universal resonance than the earth and hill symbolism of the traditional Kimbu Creator; and the conus-shells which particularly objectified that powerful symbolism spanned a vast area from the East African Coast to Lake Tanganyika, becoming in themselves the means by which alliances between chiefdoms were created and hegemonies set up. Perhaps, as Monica Wilson suggests, this theological change of scale was a step in the direction of monotheism in the sense that the supreme being in his sun aspect was essentially the giver of life to all living things, the universal providence, the overseer and judge of mankind. We thus detect in an African Traditional Religion a development of ideas and an enrichment of theology, going hand in hand with processes of organizational change, change brought about by external contacts and the interaction between African peoples. The Nyitumba Kimbu were not the only bearers of conus-shell sun symbolism to western Tanzania. Apart from the Bungu already mentioned, the Sagali group of chiefdoms in Unyamwezi also have traditions linking themselves to the westward movement from the eastern Tanzanian hinterland. The Nyitumba Kimbu, however, were especially active in distributing conus-shells to neighbouring Nyamwezi peoples in Ugalla, Ukonongo and Mpimbwe, and, consequently, in establishing a network of alliances there. Nevertheless, the conus-shell 'idea' soon leapt over the boundaries created by these alliances to be adopted by independent chiefdoms even further west, such as those of Ufipa.

5 Conclusion

The example provided by this chapter clearly shows how the disciplines of African History are able to reveal unexpected depths in the theology of African Traditional Religion. These disciplines include the examination of linguistic evidence, the study of oral, historical traditions, the analysis of myths, folk-tales, praise-names and song-texts and the observation of religious and chiefly rituals and regalia. All of these combine to give us an impressive picture of developments in religious thought in western Tanzania in the latter part of the 18th century. Given the structural and cultural similarity of the Kimbu, Nyamwezi and Sukuma peoples, this case study also takes on something of the limited comparative approach, although the emphasis has been mainly on the historical side. In the next chapter two examples of the limited, comparative approach are presented, with the emphasis placed on structural and cultural similarities and differences.

Notes

1. This chapter is based on a paper given at the Third Conference on the Historical Study of Religion, held at Limuru, Kenya in June 1974. The hypothesis of the original paper has been corrected and developed in the light of the discussion and consultation that it provoked.

2. Cf. Shorter, A., 1972, *Chiefship in Western Tanzania*, Oxford.

3. Harjula, R., 1969, *God and the Sun in Meru Thought*, Helsinki, pp. 22-30.

4. This name apparently derives from a Turu clan originating in Ufipa, according to Cory, H., no date, 'Rimi Law and Custom', unpublished typescript in the library of the Makerere Institute of Social Research, Kampala (ref. 6.5/24). The Turu have been described by Jellicoe, M., 1967a, 'Social Change in Singida', (Thesis submitted for the degree of M.A., Makerere University; 1967b, 'Praising the Sun', *Transition*, 31, vi, 6; and 1968, 'The Shrine in the Desert', *Transition*, 34, vii, 3.

5. E.g. Malachi, iii, 20: 'But for you who fear my name, the sun of righteousness will shine out with healing in its rays.'

6. Cf. Dahl, E., 1915, *Nyamwesi-Wörterbuch*, Hamburg, 637.

7. Professor Christopher Ehret, personal communication, June 1974.

8. Schönenberger, P., 1961, 'Names for God Known and Used by the Wanyamwezi', *Anthropos*, lvi, 5/6, pp. 947-949.

9. A fine example of a Kimbu ghost-horn was obtained by the author from the chief of Ilamba and presented to the National Museum of Tanzania in Dar-es-Salaam in 1968.

10. Cf. Shorter, A., 1972, *Chiefship in Western Tanzania*, Oxford, p. 108, fn. 7. Names for hills include: Igululilu, Igulwibi, Luwigulu Milungu, Magulu. Chiefdom names include: Wikangulu, Ngulu.

11. It was interesting that when I asked a Christian catechist to help me translate the Lord's Prayer, he preferred *xwilonde* to *xwigulu* for 'in heaven'.

12. Kimbu song text recorded at Mbole village, October 6th, 1965.

13. Personal communication from Mr Patrick Pender-Cudlip, June 1974.

14. Personal communication from Mr Patrick Pender-Cudlip, June 1974.

15. Cf. Shorter, A., 1972, 'Animal Marauders and Family Morality in Africa', *Africa*, xlii, 1, pp. 5-6.

16. The story was being told about 80 miles away from Chunya town, the Area Headquarters.

17. Kipembawe was a village situated about 15 miles away from Mbole where the story was told.

18. Ngwala was a village situated about 40 miles west of the story-teller's village, and Ubungu was the neighbouring tribal area to the south.

19. Story told by Mulugala Kasaka at Mbole Village, December 30th, 1969.

20. Blohm, W., 1933, *Die Nyamwezi, Gesellsschaft und Weltbild*, Hamburg, pp. 141 and 187.

21. Shorter, A., 1969, 'Religious Values in Kimbu Historical Charters', *Africa*, 3, pp. 231-237. The text of the myth is given in Shorter, A., 1972, *Chiefship in Western Tanzania*, Oxford, pp. 154-156.

22. *Ibid.*

23. Wilson, Monica, 1971, *Religion and the Transformation of Society*, Cambridge.

Chapter V

Two Examples of the Limited Comparative Approach

1 The Religion of the Nuer and Dinka of Sudan

In the first section of this chapter we examine the religions of two Nilotic peoples of Sudan, the Nuer and Dinka. These are both pastoralist, cattle-owning peoples who move according to fixed patterns with their herds in the vicinity of the White Nile and its tributaries. The two groups have been the subject of separate studies by the well-known British anthropologist, the late Sir Edward E. Evans-Pritchard and his gifted pupil, Godfrey Lienhardt. Both have written fairly extensively about their respective groups, but our attention is drawn to the two masterly monographs on their religion which rank among the finest studies of African Traditional Religion. These are: *Nuer Religion*, by Evans-Pritchard (Oxford 1956) and *Divinity and Experience: The Religion of the Dinka*, by Lienhardt (Oxford 1961). It may be that the Nuer and Dinka were in Evans-Pritchard's mind when he proposed a limited comparison between peoples possessing strong structural and cultural similarities and who are geographically contiguous. The Nuer and Dinka fulfil these conditions. They are so remarkably similar that the differences which exist between them take on a special interest, and not least among the questions that must be asked is: 'Are these few differences factual or are they the result of slightly different methodological assumptions by the two authors?' Both authors refer to the other group during the course of their studies on the religion, and in other books and articles, but neither author, as far as I know, has made an extensive attempt to compare the two. What follows in this chapter is obviously a mere sketch and on a secondary level. It is a comparison of the two religious systems as the two authors present them in their books and is not based on any first-hand information. The aim is simply to demonstrate the possibilities of the methodological proposals of Evans-Pritchard in his Hobhouse lecture.[1] A more thoroughgoing comparison is clearly demanded in the long run.

2 *The Religion of the Nuer*

Evans-Pritchard begins his discussion of Nuer religion by talking of the Nuer conception of 'God'. He is not afraid of the word 'God' and the Nuer word which he is translating is *Kwoth,* a word which literally means 'spirit'. However, he tells us at once that the word *Kwoth* is not only used with reference to God but also, in its plural form, to the 'spirits of the above' and the 'spirits of the below'. In its singular form, *Kwoth* refers to *the* spirit of the above, God. What is Evans-Pritchard's justification for isolating this spirit of the above from the other spirits of the above and for translating the term as 'God'? He offers us three main reasons:

1. The analogy between *Kwoth*/Spirit and the Latin and Greek ideas of *spiritus* and *pneuma*. These classical ideas of 'spirit' or 'breath' find their culmination in a personal God. Nuer religious thought is similar, and so their personalization of spirit can be accurately translated 'God'.

2. The spirit of the above (in the singular) is the prototype of all spirits and therefore is a necessary concept for understanding the other elements of Nuer religious belief.

3. There is evidence that the multiplicity of spirits is due to cultural contact with the neighbouring Dinka and that *Kwoth* (singular) is fundamentally a monotheistic conception.

Nuer religion is basically concerned with the problem of unity and diversity in human experience, with man's dependence on the phenomena of nature and on his fellow man coupled with his experience of separation from these phenomena and his inability to control them. Evans-Pritchard presents us with an essentially theistic picture of the spirit of the above which pervades Nuer society and which epitomizes the experience of closeness and separation. This is the paradox of the Nuer God. The various spirits which are

80

referred to in the plural form of the name are social refractions of God himself. Moreover, God, for the Nuer, is
clearly a person, a creator and in some sense a 'father' of
spirits and of men, and social analogies are used to describe
the relationship of God to other phenomena. Such social
analogies are found in Nuer mythology, and the myths
typically express the separation of God from man and the
helplessness of man.

God is associated symbolically with the sky, with the sun,
moon and astral bodies generally. He is also associated with
lightning, thunder and rain. These things are not God himself, merely modes or manifestations of him. Although the
spirits are thought of as separate from God, they, also, are
somehow modes of God. In a sense, they *are* God, but God
himself is not identifiable with any one of them. The spirits
are divided, as we have already indicated, into 'spirits of the
above' and 'spirits of the below', the former being those
closest to God. The following is a list of the 'spirits of the
above' and their associations:

Deng	—	rain ('spirit of the above and of the below')
Teny	—	sun after rain
Diu	—	sun
Col	—	rain and lightning
Rang	—	light and sunshine
Iviu	—	war
Buk	—	female spirit associated with rivers and streams; she is the mother of Deng and belongs both to the 'above' and the 'below'.

The 'spirits of the above' can enter into a special relationship with men and can possess them so that they become
charismatic prophets. *Buk* and *Col* have a general importance
to the whole of the Nuer people, but the other spirits have
a particular cult in different sections of the population. Clans
and families have a special relationship to one of the 'spirits
of the above' because the spirit in question has at one time
possessed a member of the family. *Col* is the spirit of those
struck by lightning and the *colwic* are those who have become spirits through being struck dead by lightning. When

such a death occurs in a clan, *Col* stands in a special relationship to the clan of the deceased.

The 'spirits of the below' are totemistic spirits, creatures or natural objects which are suggestive of spirit to Nuer. Sometimes new totems come into existence through an extraordinary happening which puts an individual in a special relationship with the totemic object. This happening could be an encounter with a wild animal, or a miraculous escape from danger. However, most totems are inherited and are explained etiologically with reference to a twin birth with an animal—twins being always closely linked in the Nuer mind with God. There are also various 'spirits of the below' which convey special power to doctors and diviners, to medicines and to talismans. Finally, some 'spirits of the above', like *Buk* for example, also have a 'below' capacity and there are certain tellurian 'spirits of the below', such as meteorites.

In a celebrated section on symbolism, Evans-Pritchard shows how it is a piece of poetic shorthand which appeals to the expressive quality of real experience. Twins *are* birds, because birds reproduce in a multiple way and because birds fly in the sky, the abode of God. The spear is a symbol of an individual's personality. It is also, through the spear-name, a symbol of the clan. When a cucumber is used as a sacrificial victim, the Nuer speak of it as an ox. The resemblance is conceptual, not perceptual. It means that when a cucumber replaces an ox, the rites must be performed as closely as possible to what happens when the victim really is an ox. 'A cucumber is an ox, but an ox is not a cucumber.'[2]

Another chapter discusses the ideas of 'soul', 'ghost' and 'afterlife'. However, although a man is thought to live on in his descendants there is no ancestor veneration. The afterlife is somehow a gloomy prospect, and yet, from another point of view, it is life with God. Nuer burial rites are chiefly preoccupied with the aim of separating the living from the dead and preventing the ghost of the deceased from interfering with, and causing trouble to, the living. In relating all of these beliefs to the social structure, the chapters on Spirit and the Social Order and on Sacrifice are probably the most important chapters in the book. However, these chapters depend on an understanding of the Nuer idea of sin as being essentially related to sickness and misfortune, and in Nuer sacrifice, the emphasis is on these.

The spirits are representatives or refractions of God in relation to particular activities, persons, groups and events. The notion of spirit, therefore, has a structural dimension. On the one hand, it is thought of in relation to man and the world in general as an omnipresent God. On the other hand it is thought of in relation to a variety of social groups and categories of persons, to political movements connected with prophets, to warfare, to descent groups and to ritual specialists of one kind or another. Enmity between social groups is regulated through the bloodfeud, and there are rituals of religious cleansing, reconciliation and sacrifice. The 'leopard skin priest', whose function it is to make peace between the groups, officiates and is the first to stab the sacrificial victim. The 'spirits of the above' and God, himself, are invoked, also the clan totem spirit of the 'leopard skin priest'. These are the spirits which unite the opposing groups. When, however, it is a question of an intra-clan ceremony, or when for some reason it is necessary to affirm the identity of the group performing the sacrifice, then the clan 'spirits of the below' are invoked, for example in the case of sickness and misfortune. Although such ceremonies may be personal, they have a social dimension.

In the moral order, the social structure affects the structure of religious thought. Mighty, celestial phenomena and terrible happenings like plagues and famines are attributable to God. Those which are less generalized are attributed to a particular refraction of God, or to a type of refraction which is evoked by the situation. Among these modes, or refractions, there is an increasing scale of importance. The spirits of prophets are personal and therefore less important than the spirits of clans. Prophetism is, in any case, an unstable, political factor. Fetishes or talismans and nature spirits whose powers are owned by individual specialists are also less important than the *colwic* and totemic spirits, but even these latter can change or be forgotten. The 'spirits of the above' are at the top of the hierarchy. With the scale of importance among the spirits goes a corresponding scale of importance in the rituals. The more important the spirit, the less detailed the ritual. The less important the spirit, the more absolute is the ownership of it by men and the more elaborate is the ritual.

The most important symbol of the relationship of religious belief to the social order is the role played by cattle. As bridewealth, cattle play an important role in marriage. They are therefore associated closely with the continuance of the lineage and with the contracts made between lineages. Cattle are also the chief victims in sacrifice, and consequently the means of communicating with spirit and the spirits, and the chief means of obtaining their favour and co-operation. This favour is sought particularly in social contexts in which cattle ordinarily have an importance, e.g. as bridewealth and bloodwealth in marriage and reconciliation rituals. In sacrifice there is a polarity between the piacular rite in which sin is expiated and the festive rite in which God and the spirits are made witnesses and sharers in the festivities of marriage and initiation. God is thought to be less demanding than the highly competitive lesser spirits. God already owns everything and he is satisfied with less than the spirits. Man, however, has to bargain with the lesser spirits who can demand attention and send sickness. There are no priests representing God in Nuer religion. The so-called 'leopard skin priests' are representatives of man, not of God. Nevertheless, they have their own spirit which plays its own part in the reconciliation process. Evans-Pritchard, thus, skilfully shows how the structure of belief is interwoven with Nuer social structure, and how it helps man to interpret his experience of society and the world.

3 The Religion of the Dinka

Lienhardt begins his study of the Dinka in a strikingly different way. He is determined to describe Dinka beliefs as far as possible in their own terms. This precludes speaking of 'God', or making any comparison with western terms such as *spiritus* or *pneuma*. Lienhardt does not consider himself to be a theologian. It is not his business to discover whether or not the Dinka notion of Divinity is the same as that of the Christian God. That is for theologians. All Lienhardt wants to do initially is to describe the Dinka notion. Dinka speak about *Nhialic* which means 'sky' or 'up-above'. Sometimes *Nhialic* is referred to in personal terms as creator and father. At other times the term refers to a number of spirits —a kind of being or activity which sums up the activities of a multiplicity of beings. Lienhardt, therefore, prefers not to speak of 'God', but of 'Divinity', a word which conveys both a personal being, a kind of nature or existence, and also a quality of a being. According to the context, it is more substantive or more qualitative; more personal or more general. 'Divinity' is, therefore, nearer to the Dinka word *Nhialic* than the English word 'God'.

Nhialic is even said by the Dinka to belong to a broader class of ultra-human agency which is known as *jok*. This word means 'power' and can be used to refer to any unexpected behaviour in a man or animal which might imply the manifestation of a power, for example, *Nhialic*. In its breadth of application it is similar to the notion *Kwoth* of the Nuer.

Divinity in its multiple aspect of 'divinities' can be classed into two groups which correspond to the lived experience of Dinka society. Lienhardt therefore approaches the subject, not like Evans-Pritchard, through the God or supreme spirit prototype, but through the manifold experience of the individual in Dinka society. The two groups of divinities are called by Lienhardt the 'Free Divinities' and the 'Clan Divinities', which are identified with particular experiences. The Dinka does not necessarily personalize these experiences, but he distinguishes them from Divinity itself which is an abstraction he is able to make from his experience. Divinity is therefore the ground of his experience.

The following are the 'Free Divinities':

Deng	—	associated with sky phenomena, especially rain, fertility and human procreation.
Abuk	—	the life of gardens and crops, also the wife/mother role.
Garang	—	the heat of the human body, also the father/son relationship.
Marcadit	—	the absence of the qualities represented by Divinity, viz. absence of peace, order or concord. *Marcadit* is the ground of sterility, sickness, death and misfortune.

The paradox about the last 'free divinity' is: How can he be Divinity, if he is the negation of Divinity? Lienhardt explains that Dinka do not conceive of Divinity producing order in the world from outside. Divinity is both order and disorder—experiential opposites. Divinity is apprehended through experience, and the experience of evil and misfortune are named as being the responsibility of *Marcadit*. Although evil and misfortune are signs of the absence of Divinity, they are also opportunities for restoring order and health. They are, therefore, in a strict relationship with Divinity.

The 'clan divinities' are the permanent and ideal values of clan relationships expressed in a symbolic form, a totem, living or non-living. Divinity is therefore imaged in lived social relationships, and these social relationships are lived in a religious way. For example, the 'clan divinity' *Ring*, 'flesh', is the divinity of the priestly clan, the 'Masters of the Fishing-Spear'. These masters, or arbitrators (who parallel the Nuer 'Leopard skin priests') have as their 'clan divinity' the life-force of their own flesh. This living flesh is seen as a kind of living illumination in them, the ground of truth and righteousness. Flesh is the principle of life and, according to the myth charter of the spear masters, they are intimately linked to the life and survival of the Dinka people. They are said to be the 'lamps' who radiate life and truth to other men. Their divinity, Flesh, is incarnate in them, and they are regarded as being partly divine themselves. This gives them the ability to order the whole community in peace.

Lienhardt then makes a study of prayer, symbolic action and sacrifice. Such prayer and action is thought by the Dinka to be infallible, but it operates on a level other than that of ordinary, experiential causality. A Dinka, for example, might perform a ritual in order to be rid of a disease, yet he will still attend a hospital for treatment. In fact, the ritual he has performed actually obliges him to take the necessary steps to secure treatment. If he did not, he would not be loyal to, or consistent with, himself, and with the ends of the ritual, which are the same as that of hospital treatment—a cure. The symbolic action recreates and dramatizes the circumstances which the Dinka hope to control, and his experience of these circumstances is changed by the ritual. He aims to achieve this result by operating at two levels—religious and non-religious. He therefore experiences the circumstances of his misfortune religiously, and should the ritual fail, it means that Divinity has refused the sacrifice for some reason, or that the sacrifice offered was not the one prescribed.

Although Dinka hope to control events through prayer and symbolic action, there is nevertheless a strongly expressed awareness of human weakness and dependence on unseen powers. It is through the acknowledgement of his own weakness and of the power of the divinities that he has power to control them. This is brought out well in the ritual of bloody sacrifice. Here the victim is seen both as the substitute for the sinner or sufferer who prays to be relieved of his condition, and also as an aspect of Divinity itself. The victim is pummelled and struck and threatened, and finally killed in place of the sacrificer, but it is also shown great marks of respect, and the end result of the sacrifice is thought by those who assist to be an increase of life and vitality.

The sacrifice is the essential symbol, both of the relationship of religious beliefs to the social structure and of the multiple character of experience, which is an image of Divinity. The sacrifice is a bond of union between individuals in community who are brought together and who all take their share in an elaborate division of the sacrificial animal. The sacrifice is also a mirror of the participation of many individuals and several groups in Divinity. In this segmentary society, with a minimum of political government, it is principally at the religious level that unity is experienced. One of the pre-requisites in sacrifice is the renunciation by the participants of all discords and enmity. This is both the pre-requisite and the term of the sacrifice.

In a final chapter, Lienhardt discusses the supposed burial alive of the 'Masters of the Fishing-Spear', whose death must appear to be deliberate, since it cannot be supposed that their vitality diminishes. Nor must we forget the brilliant exposition earlier in the book of the Dinka extrapolation of ideas.[3] This passage parallels, in importance, Evans-Pritchard's treatment of symbolism. Lienhardt demonstrates how the image of an internal experience is extrapolated by the Dinka from the experiencing self, and on to an external object, person, place or thing which is seen as the source of an activity which has affected him. Lienhardt succeeds in showing, in this remarkable book, how Dinka experience is the key to an understanding of their religious ideas and beliefs.

4 The Religious Systems of the Nuer and Dinka Compared

From the accounts of their religious systems it appears that the Nuer and Dinka have much in common. They have a similar interest in cattle, and their segmentary, social structure is also similar. Both of their religious systems are basically concerned with the problem of unity and diversity in human experience and both express this experience in an idea of spirit that is simultaneously one and many. It is interesting, also, that the two systems have a similar 'double-tier' classification of spirits, corresponding to general and particular experience, and that there is evidence of Dinka influence on the Nuer in this matter. In both systems there is a special clan of priest-arbitrators, although one has the impression from the Dinka account that the 'Masters of the Fishing-Spear' are slightly more institutionalized and central to the structure of Dinka belief, than the 'Leopard skin priests' are to the Nuer structures. For both Nuer and Dinka the sacrificial role of cattle is of paramount importance in the relation of experience to religious explanation or belief. Wherein, then, does any difference lie?

Probably, there is little difference between Nuer and Dinka thinking where symbolism and extrapolation of thought are concerned. Evans-Pritchard devotes considerable space to a discussion of Nuer symbolism, while Lienhardt does the same for Dinka extrapolation of ideas. These contributions have greatly assisted anthropologists in the interpretation of the thought of other African societies; so, clearly, they have a wide application which must include both Nuer and Dinka in each case. It would be surprising if it were not so. The major difference between the two books is one of approach. The two authors approach their subject in differing ways. The question has to be asked, therefore, whether these different approaches reflect a differing emphasis in the religious systems being studied, or whether they are simply the personal idiosyncrasies of the authors themselves. Both studies are structural studies and both successfully and convincingly relate religious ideas to observed behaviour and social structure. However, Evans-Pritchard is more of a theologian. He studies the content of Nuer belief before relating it to social structure and Nuer experience. Lienhardt is the phenomenologist, refusing to discuss the ideal content, apart from the experience which it is said to reflect. The effect of these different methods is certainly to depict a more personal and theistic view of the Nuer God, and a picture of Dinka religion which in Lienhardt's words, 'is rather phenomenological than theological, an interpretation of signs of ultra-human activity, rather than a doctrine of the instrinsic nature of the Powers behind the signs'.[4] It is difficult to see how, in view of the clarity and conviction of both expositions, these differing approaches are not each suited to their own material. This conclusion is reinforced by the knowledge that the multiplicity of divinities in the Nuer system is due—to some extent—to Dinka influence. In the Nuer and Dinka religions, therefore, we are looking at two similar systems with slightly differing original emphases. This difference, however, has been eroded by interaction and unilateral influence.

5 The Religion of the Kimbu and Bungu of Tanzania

In the last chapter the reader was already introduced to the Kimbu people of south-western Tanzania, their country, their way of life and their traditional religious beliefs, with special reference to the sun symbolism of God. We shall now take a brief look at their southern neighbours, the Bungu people, and discuss their relationship to the Kimbu, as a second example of what can be achieved by limited, comparative analysis.

The Bungu (or Wungu) number today some 21,000 people. Their country (which lies between latitudes 8° and 8°35′ south, and longitudes 32°35′ and 33°20′ east) is almost two thirds dense woodland, exactly similar to the woodland country of the Kimbu. However, the other third of their land is an arid plain and it is in this plain that most of the population lives. The wooded highlands of the north are divided from the southern plain by a steep escarpment, 1,500 feet high, which runs in a north-westerly direction, meeting and bordering the south-eastern shore of Lake Rukwa. This lake is subject to intense evaporation and has been known in Bungu history to disappear almost completely. The people who live in the north are hunter gatherers and shifting cultivators like their neighbours, the Kimbu. The plain dwellers are cultivators, raisers of cattle and lake fishermen.

After 1922, when gold was found in the river Lupa and other tributaries of the Songwe which flows through southern Ubungu, the area became the scene of a minor gold rush. The Bungu themselves, however, made little profit out of it and were an insignificant proportion of the labour force. Alluvial gold was worked out by the 1940s and reef mining came to an end in the 1950s. The most important outcome of the gold working was the eventual creation of Chunya District which brought administration closer to the Bungu and Kimbu.

The story of the Bungu begins with the same expedition that brought the Nyitumba to Ukimbu in the mid-eighteenth century. In that movement, there seems to have been a number of companies of 'Sagara' from eastern Tanzania. One of these settled for three years at the newly Nyitumba conquered chiefdom of Kipembawe together with their leader, Wangu. Eventually, Wangu and his followers decided to move on to the south-west and, after a short stay in the country of a people subject to the Kimbu called Pimbili, they climbed and fortified a huge hill called Kwimba which dominates the surrounding woodland area and a long stretch of Lake Rukwa's south-eastern shore. The peoples on the lake shore, the Sanganzila, were at that time dominating a number of small groups of people to the south, above and below the escarpment, all speaking local variations of the Membe language. These people were culturally superior to the Sagara newcomers, but they were unable to resist their advance. It was they who gave the name of 'Bungu' to the Sagara for the first time. It is not easy to establish exactly what happened, but it is likely that three Bungu chiefdoms developed, one centred on Kwimba above the escarpment and two below, Iwungu and Songwe respectively. The unified Ubungu begins in the last quarter of the eighteenth century, with the overthrow of the usurper of Iwungu, Mwachiluwi.

Then began the Bungu 'golden age'. After an occupation of the country by the Ngoni, who taught the Bungu new methods of warfare, Kilanga son of Ilonga became the Bungu chief, allying himself with Arab slave-traders and himself becoming a Muslim. Under Kilanga the Bungu became a rich and warlike people whose opulence excited the envy of the Nyamwezi and who even, at times, posed a threat to the most powerful chiefdom of the Nyamwezi, Unyanyembe.

All of this came to an end with Kilanga's death in battle in 1872 and with the occupation of his country by the Nyamwezi conqueror of Ukimbu, Nyungu-ya-Mawe in about 1881. Nyungu's puppet, Zunda, was confirmed by the Germans and lived until 1915, but it was decided to divide his chiefdom and revive the Udinde (Kwimba) chiefdom under the man, Wangu III, whom Zunda had ousted. Wangu died in 1908 and the British, at that time, reunified the country.

The Bungu religion resembles that of the Kimbu at a number of points, but it represents a synthesis of different elements. Coming on the same journey and from the same country of origin as the Nyitumba Kimbu, the Bungu brought with them rituals and institutions resembling those of the Nyitumba. Bungu tradition, for example, is very clear about the conus-shell disc-emblems. Their first leader, Wangu, was crowned with the conus-shell emblem, brought from Usagara, on the summit of Kwimba hill. The conus-shell (*chelungu*) is still worn by the *Mwen'Iwungu* or Chief of the Bungu at his enthronement and at times of sacrifice. This parallels Kimbu practice. Also, like the Kimbu ruler, the Bungu chief had feathers in his headdress, taken from birds that are reputedly high-flyers or far-seeing. The Bungu conus-shell is tied on with straps of leopard skin and it is passed over a black head cloth which is symbolic of rain. The Kimbu chiefs also had black feathers in their crown which were used by rain-makers.

Bungu chiefs also have a royal dance society called *ukala*, the purpose of which is to inculcate loyalty to, and respect for, the chief. This exactly parallels the Kimbu *uwuxala*, although there are differences of detail. Both the Kimbu and the Bungu versions of this dance are performed all over Ukimbu, but I never heard that the Bungu danced the Kimbu version as well as their own. Evidence suggests that the Kimbu dance is very ancient and that it probably predates the coming of the Nyitumba. The Bungu version has been developed, in all probability, from that of the Kimbu. It is interesting, however, that the Bungu are entirely ignorant of the *imbutu* or ghost-horn.

Although they lacked developed chiefly institutions, the peoples whom the Bungu found in their new country when they arrived shared some religious ideas in common with the Kimbu further north. One of these was a veneration for hills, particularly the hill of Kwimba. Wangu I made Kwimba his fortress. He also made it his rock of judgement from which he hurled his enemies down to their deaths below, and from which he, himself, was hurled together with his final victim, Changwa, who had the presence of mind to cling on to the arm that pushed him. Kwimba became, and still remains, the holiest place in Ubungu. It is on the summit of Kwimba that the territorial spirits, the spirits of departed chiefs, are venerated every year. It is quite conceivable that part of the Bungu's prestige derived from the fact that they dwelt on the sacred mountain and used it as the base from which they descended to conquer the peoples of the lake shore and plain.

The Bungu, like the Kimbu, possess a considerable mythology about hills. The stories centre chiefly on Mtánde and Sawi hills which were the judgement places of chiefs. Various chiefs are alleged to have tried to dig up these hills and transport them to the plain below. In each case they failed. The stories seem to represent a northern tradition which celebrates the failure of the southern branch to exert authority over the semi-independent Bungu of the north. They also emphasize the fact that the religious centre of the Bungu lies in the forested north, rather than in the Rukwa plain.[5]

The Bungu also know of forest spirits similar to those in the Kimbu system, especially the *izimungala*, which exactly parallel the *imadimungala* or 'masters of the animals' known to Kimbu hunter-gatherers. The veneration of ancestors at their graves and shrines in the villages remains the principal cult, however, and for most Bungu the nature spirits of the forest belong to a misty age of legend when their ancestors dwelt in, and ruled from, the north. They are certainly not a very present reality.

In spite of the conus-shell used by the Bungu chiefs and its celestial symbolism, the God-sun linkage does not seem to appear in Bungu religion at all. The supreme being is known as *Umbambe* or *Umbeta*, 'creator' and 'providence', and, unlike the situation which the Nyitumba found in Ukimbu, there was no previous tradition of sun-symbolism for the new conus-shell concept to latch on to.[6] The only celestial associations appear to be of the chief's ancestors with lightning. The word *leza* is used for the supreme being among a number of central African peoples, and it appears to refer to lightning or thunderbolts. The Bungu do not apparently apply it to the creator, but rather to their territorial spirits, the spirits of departed chiefs. These are referred to in the plural form *maleza* and this name is also given to the village which is the principal burial ground of Bungu chiefs. The Bungu rulers established their position as ritual leaders and rain-makers and they also shared the characteristics of the divine king with the chiefs of Ukimbu. As rulers, they were pledges of divine favour for their subjects, but their special province was to counteract drought and to conserve the waters of Lake Rukwa. Chief Mwachiluwi was deposed in the latter part of the eighteenth century on the occasion of the complete drying up of the lake. When the Bungu arrived in the area in the mid-eighteenth century, they found no strong traditions of chiefship among the Sanganzila and related peoples. They seem to have maintained their own patrilineal rule of succession, unlike the Nyitumba who quickly adopted the matrilineal principle that obtained in Ukimbu. The celestial symbolism of the emblems they carried with them, the conus-shells, was accommodated to the *leza* tradition and the shells themselves came to acquire a highly esoteric significance, associated with rain-making, and known virtually only to the keepers of the regalia. Among the Kimbu, Bungu regalia is frequently an object of ridicule. It is scornfully asked whether the Bungu conus-shell represents the moon, or else part of a fish's back-bone—ideas associated with the western, lake area.[7]

Summarizing the comparison between Bungu and Kimbu religion, we can say that both are centred on the veneration of territorial spirits, but that behind the Kimbu chiefly dynasty lies a richer and more complex notion of a supreme being, a notion that has developed as a result of an interaction between two peoples. In the Bungu case, there was also interaction, but the host people were less receptive to the religious symbolism of the migrants than in the Kimbu case. Other differences are traceable to differing historical experiences and to differences in geographical environment.

Notes

1. Evans-Pritchard, E. E. Y., 1965, *The Position of Women in Primitive Societies and in Our Own and Other Essays in Social*

Anthropology, London, pp. 13-36. This present chapter is based on a lecture delivered in the Sociology Department of Makerere University in 1971.

2. Evans-Pritchard, E. E. Y., 1956, *Nuer Religion*, Oxford, p. 128.

3. Lienhardt, R. G., 1961, *Divinity and Experience*, Oxford, pp. 149-151.

4. Lienhardt, *op. cit.*, p. 32.

5. These ideas were discussed in Shorter, A., 1973, (1974), 'The Rise and Decline of Bungu Power—A Forgotten Episode in the History of Nineteenth Century Tanzania', *Tanzanian Notes and Records*, no. 73, pp. 1-18.

6. Another name for the supreme being in Ubungu is *Unkinga*, which means 'preserver'.

7. The moon is associated with the west among the Kimbu. The nearest lakes to Ukimbu are also found in the west. The lakeshore peoples live principally by fishing.

Chapter VI

Establishing Categories

1 Religion as a Dimension of Life

The nature and scope of the categorical approach to the study of African Traditional Religion was outlined in Chapter Three. There, three examples were given: the categories of Joseph Goetz based on socio-psychological criteria, the more sociological categories of Mary Douglas, and the attempt to set up categories based on differing combinations of religious variables. These categories I venture to call 'prayer models' since they reflect varied approaches to 'prayer' in its truest sense—the essential disposition of the religious believer. The aim here is to spell out this last series of categories and illustrate them with reference to recorded religious texts.[1] This would constitute a further 'offering' in the search for useful categories in the study of religion in Africa.

It is a strange fact that students of religion have been so interested in the causes and consequences of religious experience that they have forgotten to study the experience itself. By and large, academics have now given up the fruitless search for the origins of religion, and if scholars of repute, like Goetz or Douglas, are discovering correlations between religion on the one hand and sociology or social-psychology on the other, it is not that they are claiming to have found the 'explanation' of religion. Religious factors interact with social and psychological factors, and each series of factors has a certain autonomy in its own sphere. Academic freedom was won after a hard fought battle with religious dogmatism and many of the academic's agnostic attitudes are part of the aftermath of this conflict. His unwillingness to give credence to the reality of religious motivations, or—at best—his lack of interest in them, are part of a tradition to which even believing men of science unconsciously subscribe. Yet, in the history and social life of Africa religious factors cannot be so easily ignored. One example concerns the provenance of the conus-shell disc-emblems used by chiefs in western Tanzania. The evidence is incontrovertible that the first Nyamwezi long distance traders who reached the East African coast did not go there to sell ivory or slaves. Nor did they undertake that long journey to obtain fire-arms, beads, bangles or any of the new, western trade goods. They faced all the hazards of the journey to the coast for one thing—the conus-shell. It was the conus-shell, symbol of their highest religious values, that they sought. Admittedly, they soon learned of the commercial value of ivory and how to dispose of war captives. They soon learned also that fire-arms and trade-goods meant military and political influence; and conus-shells were distributed by the same hands that distributed the western goods, giving to the emblems a hitherto unheard of access of secular power. But, in their origin, the conus-shell emblems were symbols of religious faith and expectation.

The lesson of the conus-shell is that it is perilous to discount religious factors, the more so when we are studying the phenomenon of religion itself. Obviously the religion of an African people is the product of innumerable, interacting elements, environmental, economic, sociological, historical, psychological and so forth, but none of these, taken singly or all together, can account for everything in the ultimate form taken by that religion. Religious experience is both the inner experience of an individual and the mutual affirmation by a community of common insights. It has to do with ordinary life, and it is to a greater or lesser extent determined by the factors of ordinary life, psychological, sociological, economic, and historical. But it is a further dimension of this life, a transcendent quality of life, which the believer is privileged to see. It is comparable to what happens when an artist, musician or dancer interprets an ordinary human experience but opens the eyes and ears of his audience, through his artistry, to new qualities in the experience which were hitherto dormant or undeveloped in their minds.

Religion, therefore, is not simply belief, or morality, or ritual, or structures. It is basically prayer—not prayer as formal communication with spiritual beings in worship— but the essential disposition of the man of faith which this worship reflects. Religious faith is the consciousness of a further dimension to life, the living communion of man with a spiritual 'world', not separate from, or opposed to, this world, but discovered and lived in this world. In Africa personalized, spiritual beings characterize the spiritual worlds of traditional religions, and in order to study an African religion, one must ask: What is the shape of this communion? What forms does the relationship take? What differences are there between man's experience of the spiritual world in his ordinary life and his attempts to establish formal contact with it in worship? Asking such questions will, in my view, take us a stage further than the levels achieved by categories such as those of Goetz and Douglas (with which I am in broad agreement). If religion is concerned with relationships, rather than with practices—and I believe it is—then, we must ask: What sort of a relationship? And with whom? And we are forced to juggle with the variables exhibited by the theologies of African religions: supreme being, divinities, ancestors, mediators and so on. Mary Douglas, through her application of Bernstein's ideas about the influence of language on culture to the influence of social experience on African ritual, has provided an advance on Goetz's simple categories of theism and deism. The following categories are a direct development of Goetz's ideas, but they also owe something to the more complex picture drawn by Douglas.

In most African Traditional theologies the idea of a supreme being is more or less distinctly present. Whether he is conceived as creator or begetter, whether or not he is a part of man's proximate experience, the idea of the supreme being is strong enough and ubiquitous enough to make nonsense of the term 'animism' which is so frequently and mistakenly applied to African religions. Coupled with the notion of supreme being are three other levels of spiritual being which we may refer to as: modes, mediators and divinities. In the first case we are speaking of something inseparable from the experience of the supreme being himself (whose unicity and unity may be only dimly or imperfectly apprehended). In the case of mediators, we are speaking of created beings who are nevertheless associated with the activity of the supreme being. Finally, in the case of divinities, we are speaking of subordinate beings, whose activity is, to a greater or lesser extent, independent of the supreme being.

97

The African traditional religionist relates to these different orders of being, both in his life-experience and in formal worship, in a limited number of different ways. Hence the models which follow.

2 Pure or Strict Theism

Using Goetz's idea of a notion of God which 'has an effective and direct influence on man's daily life'[2] and the Douglas-Bernstein picture of a 'personal religion' in an unritualistic, and unstructured or weakly structured society, we come to the first category which may be called 'pure' or 'strict' theism. In this religious situation man experiences the spiritual world in a direct and uncomplicated way. The overriding power is that of the supreme being directly present in human experience and directly approached in simple forms of worship.

A classic example of this religious type is the much studied religion of the Pygmies. Pygmy hunter-gatherers have the least structured type of society, based on the fluctuating membership of the roving band, and their worship takes the form of direct invocation of the creator and of simple—sometimes silent—offerings to him. Usually, their offerings take the form of a first-fruits oblation after the hunt or food-gathering expedition. The following prayer from the Pygmies of Gabon applies the first-fruits idea to the newborn child, here referred to as a 'new plant', which is offered to its creator.

To you the creator, to you the powerful
I offer this new plant,
New fruit of the old tree.
You are the master, we are the children.
To you the creator, to you the powerful.[3]

Another fine example of Pygmy theism is the following religious poem about the supreme being's spiritual omnipresence. In this short text the Pygmies of Zaïre refer to the supreme being as *Kmvoum*.

In the beginning was *Kmvoum*,
Today is *Kmvoum*,
Tomorrow will be *Kmvoum*.

Who can make an image of *Kmvoum*?
He has no body.
He is as a word which comes out of your mouth.
That word! It is no more.
It is past and still it lives!
So is *Kmvoum*.[4]

This type of religion may also typify some of the African pastoralist societies, and again a much quoted example is that of the Boran of northern Kenya. The following prayer for both external and internal peace illustrates well how the Boran believer encounters the supreme being directly in life and in prayer-texts like this one.

O God, thou hast let me pass the night in peace,
Let me pass the day in peace.
Wherever I may go
Upon my way which thou madest peaceable for me,
O God, lead my steps.
When I have spoken,
Keep off calumny from me.
When I am hungry,
Keep me from murmuring.
When I am satisfied,
Keep me from pride.
Calling upon thee, I pass the day,
O Lord who hast no Lord.[5]

The societies of the Kikuyu and Meru of Kenya are considerably more structured than that of the Pygmies or even that of the Boran. However, what holds their territorial clusters together is not a hierarchical or segmentary system, but a highly stratified organization of age sets and generation sets. This makes for a greater egalitarianism in their society, and for a sharing of authority in councils of elders. In the religious thought of these settled cultivators ancestral spirits play an important role, but they do not clearly fall into any of the categories that were listed above. In fact, these ancestral spirits are not apparently thought to exert a direct influence on the living, nor are they addressed in formal worship. They are the good spirits who sought and won the favour of the supreme being during their lifetimes and whose friendship with the living today is a pledge of future blessings. The supreme being, *Ngai*, who dwells on the shining mountain (*Kere-Nyaga*, or *Kenya*) is favourably disposed towards his children when he sees their filial piety towards their ancestors, and their anxiety to do the things that they did. The following Kikuyu prayer for the blessing of a new homestead is typical of the desire to be 'in harmony with the spirits of our ancestors', but it exhibits the same basic theism as the other societies we have been considering.

You the Great Elder, who dwells on the Kere-Nyaga,
Your blessing allows homesteads to spread.
Your anger destroys homesteads.
We beseech you, and in this we are in harmony
With the spirits of our ancestors;
We ask you to guard this homestead and let it spread.
Let the women, herd and flock be prolific.
Chorus:
Peace, praise ye Ngai,
Peace be with us![6]

3 Modes of Existence of the Supreme Being

Mary Douglas rightly places the Nuer and Dinka of Sudan among societies that are weakly structured. She goes even further than this and in an interesting analysis of the contrasting Nuer and Dinka attitudes to prophetism, attributes Dinka tolerance towards people in a state of trance to the fact that their society is even more weakly structured than that of the Nuer.[7] Our discussion, in Chapter Five, of the religions of these two societies can scarcely leave us in any doubt that they fit Goetz's category of theism. However, this theism is of a more subtle and complex kind. As we have seen, both of these societies describe a spiritual power that is both personal and supreme, but which is imaged in a variety of spirits which reflect the multiplicity of human experience. These spirits are not conceived as being independent, or even distinct entities. Rather, they are 'refractions', modes or qualities of the supreme being. Using Lienhardt's terminology, Divinity and the divinities are experienced together and worshipped together. The following text illustrates this. In this prayer for rain, the free divinity, Deng, is mentioned in the same breath with Divinity. (The 'black bull' released from the 'moon's byre' refers to the clouding over of the penumbra of the moon.)

> Great Deng is near, and some say 'far'.
> O Divinity,
> The Creator is near,
> And some say 'he has not reached us'.
> Do you not hear, O Divinity?
> The black bull of the rain
> Has been released from the moon's byre,
> Do you not hear, O Divinity?[8]

Goetz demonstrates convincingly how sky symbolism is associated with theistic belief, and this is certainly true of the Nuer and Dinka.[9] For the Bushmen of South Africa, celestial symbols play an important role in expressing their religious experience and expectations. Among the heavenly bodies, the Moon has a particular importance. Its relationship to the sky-god himself is expressed in the form of a myth: the moon is the creator's 'shoe', but it is the moon which figures in most of the texts as the source of material success—chiefly in hunting—and of eternal life beyond the grave. Once again, we are dealing with a hunting-gathering society comparable in some ways to the Pygmies and weak in both group-centred and ego-centred social relationships. The following is a Bushman prayer for immortality.

> Take my face and give me yours!
> Take my face, my unhappy face.
> Give me your face,
> With which you return
> When you have died,
> When you vanished from sight.
> You lie down and return—
> Let me resemble you, because you have joy,
> You return evermore alive,
> After you vanished from sight.
> Did you not promise me once
> That we too should return
> And be happy again after death?[10]

4 Symmetrical Mediation

The concept of mediators belongs to a world that is at once more settled and more strongly structured than the societies we have just been considering. Perhaps the word 'mediator' is a misleading one, suggesting, as it does, the role of an intercessor familiar to the Christian in the doctrine of the communion of saints. The idea of spirit-intercessors is not entirely foreign to the theologies of African Traditional Religion, and the Bemba of Zambia have a custom which dramatizes such a belief, whispering messages to the supreme being and to their departed loved ones into the ear of a corpse before burial. Be that as it may, the idea of mediation in African religion is more dynamic and vital. It owes more to the concept of intermediary than to the concept of messenger or spokesman. Intermediaries play an important role in numerous situations in this kind of society, particularly when marriage negotiations between two family communities are taking place. The intermediary is consulted and briefed by both parties, but commitments made to the intermediary are considered as binding as if they had been made directly between the parties themselves. The intermediary is not considered to be a barrier to communication, rather he is an essential channel of communication at solemn and important moments of social life. It is not difficult, let alone contradictory, therefore, for an African traditional religionist to see his experience of, and communication with, the supreme being as channelled almost exclusively, if not exclusively, through spirit-mediators. In our earlier discussion of the religion of the Kimbu of Tanzania, we examined the way in which their understanding and symbolism of the supreme being developed as a result of historical factors. It is important to grasp the fact that, while this idea of the supreme being is rich and complex, it was not traditionally separate from the idea of the chief and his ancestors, the territorial spirits, as intermediaries of the supreme being. The supreme being was believed to be the ultimate source of all blessings, rain, good harvests, plentiful meat and honey, victory in war, peace at home and so forth, but all of these benefits were mediated through divinely constituted intermediaries. On earth, the reigning chief was the visible guarantor of prosperity, but even he was merely the 'vicar' of the territorial spirits.

His ambivalent position was symbolically expressed by his role at the time of offering to his ancestors. He could not make offerings himself; nor could he go with the sacrificers to the graveside. Instead, he remained seated in his house, wearing his regalia, in silent communion with his ancestors, while the ghost-horn, blown from inside his house all the way to the grave-shrine and back, formed the symbolic link. I once asked an elderly Kimbu informant why the Kimbu prayed to ancestors, rather than to the supreme being. My informant was surprised. 'But the ancestors *are* the supreme being,' he replied. To my further question whether the ancestors were not creatures of the supreme being, he replied, 'Yes, of course. They were created by him.'

In what way does the Kimbu statement: 'the ancestors are the supreme being' differ from the Nuer statement: 'the spirits are God'? I think in this, that the ancestors are not only thought of as being separate from the supreme being although in some way identifiable with him, but this separation consists in their status as created beings who lived an historical life on earth and who maintain solidarity with their descendants. Their relationship to the supreme being is not that of a mode or quality; it is the same kind of mysterious link as the link between the divine king or chief and his predecessors. They are separate beings having a mystical unity. The Kimbu does not pray to the supreme being; he prays to territorial spirits and ancestors. However, he does address the supreme being—always in the third person—in a form of declaratory oath by which he calls him to witness the faithful accomplishment of his duty of offering or prayer. '*Ilyuva* has seen it!' is the invariable formula which concludes a prayer to the ancestors.

I believe that the Kimbu model is fairly widespread in Africa, particularly among the multi-chiefdom societies of Eastern Africa. Prayer texts are not, perhaps, very revealing in this category, since—as we shall see—they need not exhibit any significant difference from texts belonging to the next category. Here, however, is one from the Tumbuka people of Malawi, a form of confession for sin during an influenza epidemic. The text reflects a religious situation similar to that of the Kimbu in which the 'great ones' or territorial spirits mediate both the experience of the supreme being's causality and man's worship of the supreme being.

Let the great ones gather!
What have we done to suffer so?
We do not say, 'Let so-and-so come',
We say 'all'.
Here your children are in distress.
There is not one able to give a drink of water to another.
Wherein have we erred?
Here is food; we give to you.
Aid us, your children! [11]

5 Asymmetrical Mediation

This category is possibly even more common than the last,
since it relates to societies with a less ritualized form of
chiefship. According to this model, the mediators are mainly
thought to be channels of prayer. As in the last model, they
are somehow identifiable with the supreme being, 'in his
arms', as the Mende of Sierra Leone put it. On the other
hand, the influence of the supreme being is felt directly and
he is even prayed to on occasion. The mediators are not,
therefore, the exclusive intermediaries for the whole of man's
dealings with the supreme being that they were in the last
category. The following prayer of the Luguru of Tanzania
affords an example of prayer addressed both to the supreme
being and to the ancestors.

You, Father God,
Who are in the heavens and below;
Creator of everything, and omniscient
(Of) how the earth and the heavens (were made).
We are but little children
Unknowing anything evil;
If this sickness has been brought by man,
We beseech thee, help us through these roots!
In case it is inflicted by you, the Conserver,
Likewise do we entreat your mercy on your child;
Also you, our grandparents who sleep in *kutzimu* (Hades),
We entreat all of you, sleep on one side.
All ancestors, male and female, great and small,
Help us in this trouble, have compassion on us;
So that we can also sleep peacefully,
And hither do I spit out this mouthful of water!
Pu-pu! Pu-pu!
Please listen to our earnest request! [12]

The following invocation from the Mende of Sierra Leone also addresses both supreme being and ancestors (*Kenei Momo* and *Nduawo*). Paradoxically, the supreme being is asked to let the prayer reach the ancestors, although it is the ancestors who are the intermediaries. This text demonstrates the idea of the closeness between ancestors and the supreme being very well.

> O God, let it reach to *Kenei Momo*,
> Let it reach to *Nduawo*,
> Let it reach to all our forefathers
> Who are in your arms.[13]

6 Relative Deism

Seeking to define deism, Goetz has recourse to Diderot's classic definition: 'a concept of God which has no religious reality'.[14] This is an excellent, if succinct, definition; it is also a definition of an extreme case. In labelling some traditional African theologies as deistic, I am not at all anxious to empty them of all religious reality. However, there obviously are many religious systems in Africa in which, not only is the supreme being not directly experienced by the believer, but the supreme being has a tense and equivocal relationship with other divinities or spirits. Direct worship of the supreme being may still take place, or, as is the case with the Yoruba of Nigeria, it may have taken place until fairly recent times. The problem is one of the connection between the worship of the supreme being (who is not necessarily in these systems the creator) and the worship of the other divinities. The latter represent many different facets of human experience and social life and they are the objects of well established local cults, each with their own shrines and shrine-keepers or priests. The divinities cannot simply be classified as mediators in the sense in which this term has been used above. They are not mere intercessors, nor are they active intermediaries. Their relationship towards the 'king' of the divinities or towards the creator, if the latter concept is not separate from the former, may be intimate, but it is also thought to be tense. This may be expressed, as among the Yoruba, by myths of rebellion and warfare between the divinities and their king. Such myths may ultimately serve a tradition about the latter's supremacy, but, in the presence of strongly established local cults, this tradition may be no more than a belief and so lend substance to Diderot's definition. At other times, as among the Ganda of Uganda, although creation myths establish a logical and chronological priority of the creator-spirit over the other nature spirits and heroes, the strength of local traditions may have obscured this fact. Several times I have assisted at fascinating, but unresolved, discussions between Ganda university lecturers and graduates as to whether the creator (*Katonda*) was supreme among the divinities (*Lubaale*), or not. That such discussions can take place seems to me to be another argument in favour of Diderot.

Mary Douglas describes a type of society which seems to correspond to this theological model. It is a type of society in which there is less emphasis on group loyalties, and greater importance is attached to the ways in which the individual relates to others in categories focused on himself. Social esteem based on individual success and achieved rank and status seem to be important in this situation, and this may harmonize well with a hierarchical society or centralized kingdom in which government is carried on through appointed officers rather than through families or clans possessing a particular social role. It is also a type of society which enjoys an advanced material culture and in which material things may sometimes be more dominant than persons. The cosmos can, according to this way of thinking, be manipulated by means of impersonal forces such as *juju*, or through individual, magical objects. As an example of the latter, I would propose the Ganda *mayembe* or spirit horns, objects through which spirits can be approached and even conjured into one's power. There are many societies which fit this category: some of the other Bantu peoples of southern and western Uganda, the Akan, Ga and Ewe of Ghana, the Ibo, Yoruba and Nupe of Nigeria and probably many others. A single text, whether it be addressed either to the supreme being or to one of the divinities cannot be expected to reveal very many aspects of this model. However, in view of the crucial relationship between divinities and supreme being, the following Yoruba hymn bears a special interest. According to Professor E. B. Idowu, it is the hymn which the divinities—according to tradition—sang after their rebellion against the king of the divinities, *Olódùmarè* or

Edùmarè. Having usurped the latter's place, they brought the world to a standstill and were forced to acknowledge his superior power. It remains a fact, however, that the divinities are worshipped, while the cult of *Olódùmarè* has fallen into abeyance.

> Be there one thousand four hundred divinities of the home,
> Be there one thousand two hundred divinities of the market place,
> Yet there is not one divinity to compare with *Olódùmarè.*
> *Olódùmarè* is the king unique.
> In our recent dispute,
> *Edùmarè* it is who won.
> Yes, *Edùmarè.*[15]

7 *Pure or Strict Deism*

Is it possible to find among the Traditional religions of Africa a system in which Diderot's definition is fulfilled to the letter, viz. one in which the concept of the supreme being is completely devoid of all religious reality? Given the proverbial religiosity of the African, one might think not. However, there is at least one candidate that is seriously proposed. This is the Acholi people of the Central Luo group in Uganda. At first sight, the Acholi religion bears some resemblance to that of their cousins, the northern Nilotes across the Uganda-Sudan border, the Nuer and Dinka. Like the latter, the Acholi have a generic term for spirit which stands both for the many and for the one—*Jok*. There are *Joks* corresponding to different levels of human and social experience, but without doubt, the most important is that of the territorial or chiefdom *Jok*, to whom offerings and prayers are regularly made at specified shrines. The question is: Does the word *Jok* in its generic form correspond to any personalized, supreme being, as is the case with the Dinka and Nuer of Sudan? Dr Okot p'Bitek, the well-known writer and satirical poet, and himself an Acholi, answers confidently in the negative. I once had the privilege of attending a lecture given by him at Makerere University with the provocative title: 'Is *Jok* God?' The vehemence with which his negative answer was rejected by a large section of the audience, all Acholi like himself, was a clear indication that his opinion is not widely shared. Chesterton once unkindly dismissed the poet and novelist Thomas Hardy as 'the village atheist writing about the village idiot', but it would be patently unjust to accuse Dr Okot p'Bitek of atheistic bias in his various literary excursions into the Acholi rural scene, although he seems to be a determined agnostic. The facts about the religion of the Acholi are sufficiently obscure and difficult to interpret, that the question of *Jok*'s identity must remain open.

I have suggested, in a review of Dr Okot p'Bitek's book on the religion of the Central Luo, that we might be mistaken in assuming that there must be an overall, unified religious system for all the Acholi chiefdoms.[16] Might it not be the case that each Acholi chiefdom is, as it were, a cosmos of its own, with its own chiefdom *Jok* at the centre of this cosmos? Much would depend, in this case, on how fragmented the different political sections of the Acholi traditionally were. If there is some truth in this hypothesis, then the problem of *Jok* is a modern problem, the product of enlargement of social scale and social incorporation in recent times. Even if Dr Okot p'Bitek is wrong, the religious content of the generic term *Jok* certainly remains a mystery, and so weak a concept as to justify the description of 'pure' deism.

It should be noted that the Acholi outlook is not a secularist or unreligious, unritualistic outlook, although one can agree with Mary Douglas that such an outlook is not unknown among some African peoples. The Acholi do very clearly believe in a living communion with spirits and their worship is organized both on a personal and on a territorial basis. Mary Douglas identifies a type of society in which group loyalties are very strongly experienced and in which there is a dual philosophy of warring forces of good versus evil, the evil being represented mainly as witchcraft. Apart from the fact that it is extremely doubtful whether the Acholi have this degree of cohesion and witchcraft domination, it is not possible to establish this kind of dualism at the level of experiential prayer or in relation to spiritual beings. Although he possesses praeternatural powers, the witch in Africa still remains a human being and is dealt with in the context of social control or magical techniques, rather than of religious belief and worship. It is in the more recent millennarian, witch-eradication movements that forms of religious protection and retaliation have come to the fore, and these have characterized Central Africa where Mary Douglas finds examples of this dualistic category. The only possible case of a theological dualism known to me is that of the Luyia of Kenya with their 'white god' (*Ratsari*), and their 'black god' (*Wele Gumali*), but I am not sure whether this should provide a basis for yet another religious category.[17] To conclude this section and the chapter as a whole, we give a prayer text addressed by Acholi to a chiefdom *Jok*.

Jok of our chiefdom,
Jok of our forefathers.
We have brought food for you.
We have brought chicken and goat.
We have brought termite and butter.
Our insides are clean;
We have brought you food with clean insides,
Eat it.
We have brought you children,
Here they are.
We beseech you, Oh!
Let your children have childbirth.
Untie the young women
So that childbirth may fall on them.
The little girls are here,
Let them develop breasts.
You *Joks* of our chiefdom,
Let the crops yield,
The rains fall peacefully.
Let the children have good health.
The sicknesses that are coming,
Let them pass far away.[18]

Notes

1. These categories were first put forward in Shorter, Aylward, 1974, *Prayer in the Religious Traditions of Africa*, Nairobi. This chapter presents them in a much fuller and more detailed discussion. In the book the categories were used to introduce a collection of prayer-texts.

2. Goetz, Joseph (with Bergounioux, F. M.), 1965, *Prehistoric and Primitive Religions*, London, p. 80.

3. Anonymous, 1962, 'Structures fondamentales de la prière Négro-

Africaine', in *Personnalité Africaine et Catholicisme (Présence Africaine)*, Paris, pp. 91-137.

4. Young, T. C., 1940, *Contemporary Ancestors*, London, p. 23.

5. Tutschek, C., 1845, *A Grammar of the Galla (Boran) Language*, Munich, pp. 87-88.

6. Kenyatta, J., 1938, *Facing Mount Kenya*, London, pp. 81-82.

7. Douglas, Mary, 1970, *Natural Symbols*, London, pp. 86-95.

8. Nebel in Schmidt, W., 1949, *Der Ursprung der Gottesidee*, Vol. VIII, p. 143.

9. Cf. Goetz, *op cit.*, pp. 69-81, and above, Chapter Five.

10. Schmidt, W., 1933, *Der Ursprung der Gottesidee*, Vol. VI, p. 557.

11. Young, T. C., 1950, 'The Idea of God in Northern Nyasaland', in Smith, E. W. (ed.) *African Ideas of God*, London, p. 44.

12. Mawinza, J., 1968, 'Reverence for Ancestors in Tanzania, with Reference to the Luguru and other Bantu tribes', in *Theory and Practice in Church Life and Growth* (mimeographed), Nairobi, p. 45.

13. Harris, W. T., 1950, 'The Idea of God Among the Mende', in Smith, *op cit.*, p. 201.

14. Goetz, *op. cit.*, p. 80.

15. Idowu, E. B., 1962, *Olódùmaré, God in Yoruba Belief*, London, p. 55.

16. *Azania*, Volume VII—1972, pp. 190-193.

17. Wagner, G., 1954, 'The Abaluyia of Kavirondo', in Forde, D. (ed.), *African Worlds*, Oxford, p. 44.

18. Okot p'Bitek, 1971, *The Religion of the Central Luo*, Nairobi, p. 69. It is in this book that the author also puts forward his understanding of *Jok*.

Chapter VII

The Study of Themes in African Traditional Religion

1 The Importance of Themes

Much of the writing about African Traditional Religion is purely descriptive, and it is unhappily rather rare to find attempts at penetrating beyond the externals. There are few works of serious interpretation to compare with a book like that of Lienhardt on Dinka religion.[1] In the syllabuses and examination papers of University and Seminary African Theology courses one finds an emphasis on what might be called 'concreteness'—on concrete institutions, rituals, sacred objects and buildings, cultic roles, personalized spiritual beings and so forth.[2] There is comparatively little attention paid to values and to themes. Yet values and the themes through which they are expressed are the most important and most lasting elements in African Traditional Religion. Long after the visible aspects of African Religion have disappeared and the cults and practices have ceased to be performed, the values, and even many of the themes, survive in the minds and hearts of men who may have adopted one of the immigrant religions, or who have no religious practice at all. There are grounds for expecting that such religious themes and values will continue to form part of popular culture for a long time to come. In a true dialogue between religious traditions—a veritable meeting of meanings—we are, of course, dealing mainly with themes and values.

What do we mean by the words: 'value' and 'theme'? Put very simply, value is the worth which we ascribe to a choice —choice of an object, an opinion, a course of action, a relationship, a role, an experience. In a choice one alternative is preferred to others (or another), and a worth is conferred upon it. What this alternative is worth to us is its 'value', and it takes its place in a hierarchy of values, relating to the

111

various alternatives and the various levels of choice. In Africa, it is often said, the parental aspect of marriage is more important than the conjugal aspect. Here we have an African value. In many African societies consumption confers prestige, rather than conservation of wealth. This would be another value.

Values are expressed as a repeated and consistent *leitmotiv* in any number of contexts, through any number of images or symbols. They become a regularity or pattern in the thought of a people or culture. In this case we would call them 'themes'. Some themes are particular to a culture, but others are what might be called 'life-themes' since they relate to universal human experience. Such life-themes would include attitudes to the basic experiences and crises of human life: birth, puberty, marriage, sickness and health, old age, death, friendship, alienation, happiness, sorrow, work, leisure and so on. Some life-themes refer to explicit religious experience, for example: human inadequacy and sin, the experience of God, creation and creativity, judgement, salvation—to name only a few examples. Different cultures have different approaches to these themes, and even if they have identical or similar approaches, they may express these approaches through different sets of images and symbols.

This is not the place to go into the whole question of the structural analysis of symbols in African traditional literature and ritual. We are indebted to Claude Lévi-Strauss and Victor Turner, especially in this field, for the contributions they have made.[3] Their analytical concepts have provided social anthropologists with the tools for 'cracking the cultural code' of African symbol systems, and for discovering the underlying themes and values. Their techniques are a prerequisite for the study of religious themes in African tradition and for interpreting oral texts and ritual action in which the themes are to be found. We are concerned here with what happens after the themes have been elicited from the cultural material.

In Chapter Three we already described the thematic approach to the comparative study of African religious systems, giving as an example the work of Rev. Harry Sawyerr of Sierra Leone.[4] The purpose of this chapter is twofold. Firstly, the aim is to illustrate further this thematic approach with reference to religious themes other than that of the idea of God. Secondly, the aim is to demonstrate the richness and superiority of many African religious themes. Many times I have encountered Christians, lecturers and writers, who have asserted that such and such a theme is not present in African religious tradition, and who have gone on to claim it as a unique appendage of Christianity. My study of African religion, and, in particular, of the prayer literature of African religion, convinces me that there are more Christian themes in African Traditional Religion than one might suspect. These themes are stated in African symbolic and ritual language, and they refer to the African experience of them, but they are nonetheless authentic and superior. How right Paul VI was to say that Africa possesses values which can 'find in Christianity and for Christianity, a true superior fulness'. Christian evangelization consists not only in proclaiming, but also in listening—listening to the prophetical voice of Africa—so as to know what Christ is saying to us in the African cultures, as well as in the cultures of the Bible. Christians believe that Christ proclaims an ideal, but this ideal is no longer to be lived according to the defunct Biblical cultures. It must be rediscovered and developed within our contemporary cultures of Africa.

2 Memorial

The idea of memorial is so closely connected with the historical aspects of the Judeo-Christian tradition that it is often assumed to belong to it exclusively. Judaism and Christianity are essentially historical religions, living and celebrating the divine plan of salvation as it unfolds in human history. For Jews, as for Christians, there have been certain decisive events in that history, events of great religious significance, because they were a direct experience of divine election and deliverance. For the Jews the decisive event was the Exodus, the deliverance of the chosen people from Egyptian bondage, their being welded together as a nation and their conquest of the promised land. This great instance of God's salvific power the Jews celebrated annually in the Passover meal, an ancient first-fruits ritual which took on an entirely new meaning as a result of the historical reference. Henceforward the Passover became the most important Jewish ceremonial. During the meal, by means of specially prescribed foods and the repeated cups of wine, the minute details of that historic deliverance were recalled. However, it was not a mere commemoration in the way that a victory, or a college foundation or a birthday is commemorated. That is to say, it was not an intentional commemoration only. It was also an effective or real commemoration, because the Jews believed (and still believe) that this re-enactment of the most decisive event in their history is itself salvific. The celebration of the Passover is itself a channel of God's strength and salvation.

This concept of effective commemoration is what is called —especially by Christian writers and theologians—'memorial' or 'anamnesis', the latter being derived from a Greek word which means remembrance. Memorial or anamnesis therefore, is more than a sign of present, divine salvific power; it is an appeal to this power through the remembrance of a specific, historic event. Since the contribution of Odo Casel, the German liturgist (died 1948), the theological implications of anamnesis have been much discussed, but for Christians the idea is centred on the celebration of Word and Sacrament, and, in particular, the unique coming together of Word and Sacrament, the Eucharist. In the Eucharist there is a real and effective memorial or remembrance of the decisive, Christian facts of redemption, the life, death and resurrection of Jesus Christ. This celebration was actually instituted by Christ, himself, within the framework of the Jewish Passover with the explicit injunction to his followers: 'Do this in remembrance of me'. The Christian, therefore, believes that through obeying this command, through recalling the events of Christ's life, death and glorification, and through rehearsing the very account of the Eucharistic institution itself, he is in contact with the life-giving mystery of Christ, and with all that led up to it and all that flows from it. Memorial, therefore, not only looks backward to significant events of history; it also looks forward full of hope, because of the pledge constituted by the re-enactment of a past event. In the case of Judaism and Christianity, so-called 'historical religions', the past events are remembered in great detail, with the aid of a written tradition, although we are fast learning that none of the documents that make up the Old and New Testaments are to be treated as historical in a scientific sense. Moreover, the future hope of Jews and Christians is also fairly well delineated, in the shape of an 'end' or a 'parousia'—an eschatological fulfilment at the end of time. This will be the culmination of all human history in the Lord of History who is God himself.

Part of the refusal to credit African religions with any similar concept of memorial derives from the static and anti-historical approach of many scholars. Once it is established that African Traditional Religion has a history, and that this history can be known, the next most obvious question to ask is: Does this history have any religious significance to the traditional religionists themselves? And: Is there an authentic concept of memorial in African Traditional Religion?

Although some qualifications must be made, it would seem that the answer to both these questions is in the affirmative. The history of African religions is not so accurately or completely known, perhaps, as the history of religions in literate societies, although much of the literary material from which historical evidence is drawn is of the same kind as that found in the scriptures and holy books of peoples with a written literature. It is highly symbolical, with the historical elements subordinated to the teaching of a living faith. Moreover, African religions are not typically 'historical religions' in the sense that faith and worship are focused on certain, historical events, regarded as being of decisive importance and of great religious significance. Exceptions there certainly are, in which—as we shall see—specific historical events are remembered and celebrated; but, on the whole, history plays a less specific, though nonetheless real, part in the African religious consciousness. Again, the idea of a future culmination is more or less consistently absent from African religious speculation, although the hope for salvation in the present and the future is definitely there. Memorial in the African religious context means primarily a significant continuity with the past which provides an understanding of the present and which is the basis for a future hope.

Let us first take a look at some rather exceptional cases where specific historical events of religious significance are remembered and celebrated. In the case of the Luo of Kenya and Northern Tanzania, we have a people with a long history of migration from the southern Sudan, through present day Uganda to their actual homeland. This migration or wave

115

of migrations began at the end of the 15th century and did not come to an end until the first half of the 17th century. It was, therefore, a very important part of their historical experience—even a decisive one for their actual identity and geographical situation. In fact, as Prof. Ogot observes, Luo beliefs and religious practices cannot be understood without reference to their migrations and settlement.[6] The battles which the Luo fought with peoples on their way to the Victoria Nyanza lakeshore and in the vicinity of the lake itself gave their religion a new dimension. The spirits of strangers killed in battle were regarded as especially dangerous or powerful, and as having power to possess the living and control them. In addition the Luo have spirits associated with historical calamities. Their religion is, therefore, a guide to Luo history, and itself remains incomprehensible without this historical reference.

Another East African people with the tradition of an exodus are the Bantu-speaking Meru of Kenya. According to their traditions, they lived at one time on an off-shore island at the coast. At the dawn of their history they forded the sea channel that separated them from the mainland and began their long journey into the interior to the hills and valleys north-east of Mount Kenya which they now occupy. The Meru were led by a prophet-leader who prayed to the supreme being at the epic moment of the crossing. This beautiful prayer has been remembered by the Meru and handed down as part of their own religious tradition.[7]

The Ganda of Uganda also have a religious veneration for certain historical personalities. These have become divinities and their cult is centred on certain shrines where their relics are preserved. One such divinity is Kintu, the first king, who is alleged to have taught the Ganda the elements of their religion and a very high respect for all forms of life. His personal example had a deep and lasting influence on his community, and after his death his spirit was held to be alive. Through the religious assemblies that took place at his shrine in Singo, rules of social conduct were established and taught, and they were also occasions for prayer, sacrifice and religious songs.

However, as we have already said, such cases of an explicit appeal to historical events and personalities are probably rare in African religion. What is much more common is a general reference and sense of continuity which renders prayer and moral action effective. The Kikuyu of Kenya, in particular, are very conscious of the need to be in harmony with their ancestors and to continue the religious traditions handed down from them. It is necessary to praise the supreme being in the very same way that their forefathers praised him, and to carry out the sacrifices and other rites in the sacred places established by the ancestors—in the same groves and under the very same trees. This imitation of the ancestors, the friends of the supreme being and favoured by him, is a guarantee of future divine favour. The supreme being heard the prayer of the ancestors; he will now hear the prayer of their descendants, because it is in harmony with the ancestral prayer.[8]

Kikuyu religion has a markedly theistic emphasis. Another theistic approach to memorial is that of the Dinka of Sudan. The invocations recorded by Lienhardt reveal an attitude that is somewhat similar to that of the Kikuyu.[9] The ancestors are bidden to join in the prayer of the living, and the prayer itself may be the prayer of a prominent ancestor—an ancient prayer, a 'prayer of the long, distant past'.[10] As such it is not simply 'a prayer of the tongue', but an effective prayer, to which an answer is guaranteed.

In the religious systems in which intermediaries play an all-important role, prayer is typically addressed *to* the ancestors, rather than *with* the ancestors. Here the appeal is not to 'the long, distant past', but to the immediate past— the fidelity and the piety of the living and the duties of the parental generation, now deceased. Among the Nyoro of Uganda and the Edo of Benin, Nigeria, the argument in prayer is much the same. It runs as follows: 'You, our ancestors enjoyed life, let us enjoy it also. We have been faithful in making our offerings to you; look after us in your turn. You were good parents, caring for your children; continue to care for us now.' Of course, such appeals to the past belong more to what might be called the micro-history of the worshipper, rather than the macro-history of a people as a whole, but, limited as they are, they are still instances of the theme of memorial. In this less spectacular sense, the theme of memorial is probably very widespread indeed among African religious traditions.

3 Co-Creativity

The idea of co-creativity, man's share in the creative activity of God himself, is not only a very Christian idea; it is a Christian idea that has come into prominence in recent years. Part of the imagined incompatibility between religion and science or of Christian opposition to theories like that of evolution, was due to an inadequate understanding of the doctrine of creation. Christians in the past tended to think of creation as static, and of man's technological advances as somehow opposed to God's perfect creation. It is the attitude reflected in the old-fashioned statement: 'If God had intended us to fly, he would have given us wings!'

Today we see things very differently. Creation is not seen as static. On the contrary, God has created a world that is coming into being, and coming into being through and for man. Man's achievements are not opposed to God's creative activity. On the contrary, man exercises his talents in obedience to a primordial command to subject the earth to himself, to govern it and to make it fruitful. By his labour and by the exercise of his talents, man is unfolding the Creator's work and helping in the realization of the divine plan. Through the subjection of all things to man, they are subjected, further, to God. Through the human development of creation, the humanizing of created things, they are destined to reach fulfilment in God. The fact that man has 'come of age', that he has now mastered created things as never before, is not a matter for sorrow, but rather for rejoicing, although man is capable of deflecting himself and the things he uses from their true end in God, and this remains an ever present temptation and threat.

It has become a commonplace of popular, theological anthropology, to label all the religions of pre-literate societies as 'magical', accusing them of taking a 'sacral' attitude to created things. This is to credit traditional religions with the same kind of misunderstanding of divine creative activity as that from which the Christian West is just emerging. It is a new form of ethnocentrism in which the development of non-western societies is judged according to the recent experience of the western world. It is held that, because of western technological advance man now finds religion irrelevant, and that he must now discover God in a secular world, in the work of man's own hands. Doubtless, this is very true, but it is dangerous to go a step further and say that where technology has not advanced, i.e. in the non-western world, there is no idea of man sharing in the creative activity of God, or even to say that there is no experience of secularism. There are societies—African societies among them—which have a poorly developed technology, but which nonetheless have a man-centred cosmology, according to which men, through magical or other means, believe that they are able to control their environment with relatively little need for religious activity in the strict sense. Moreover, as we are now concerned to show, there are ideas of co-creativity, present in some African religions.

In African Traditional Religion the idea of man sharing in God's creative action is not necessarily linked to a sophisticated understanding of creation itself. Not all African peoples have a clear idea of creation, and it is usually an attribute based on the image of the human craftsman rather than a philosophical concept of creation *ex nihilo*. Creation is essentially an aspect of the supreme being's mastery over man and his world. To what extent does African religion see creation as a developing reality? To what extent does the African see the divine mastery as an on-going, developing reality? There is not, as we have seen above, any clear sense of a culmination of history, or of an accumulation of human knowledge and techniques. Man's position as 'the priest of creation' and his God-given role of taming and humanizing created nature is felt and expressed in various ways, but it is not seen as an expanding programme of world conquest. African religious systems did not possess the requisite social or theological scale for such an idea. However, there is a genuine faith in the continuity of creation, understood in this sense of divine mastery and providence, and there is also the clear conception of man's share in this continuous work. It is especially in the area of life and the transmission of life that man is thought to participate in the divine action, and it may be that ideas of co-creativity belong more to the symbolism of the supreme being as life-giver than to his symbolism as craftsman-creator.

One of the most touching examples is provided by a religious poem from Rwanda. Although it is not technically a lullaby, it is nevertheless a song sung by a mother to her child, carried on her back, to soothe and quieten it. These songs are a genre of their own in Rwanda, and they are very often deeply religious in outlook, calling upon the name of the supreme being, *Imana*. In this song the mother describes her child as 'child of my mother' and even 'mother', because it is a nominal reincarnation of its grandmother. She prays for more babies to carry on her back, and finally she hushes her child, calling him the 'field that we share with *Imana*'. In other words, she sees the child as a field that both she and the supreme being are cultivating together. Just as *Imana* gave her the child through human intercourse, so *Imana*, through human parental care, will rear the child.

Hush, child of my mother,
Hush, hush, O my mother!
God who gave you to me,
If only I could meet him,
I would fall on my knees and pray to him,
I would pray for little babies,
For little babies on my back.

You came when the moon was shining,
You came when another was rising.
Hush, field that we share,
That we share with *Imana*!
God who gave you to me,
May he also bring you up for me.[11]

The idea of co-creativity in African religious thinking is not, however, limited to the area of the transmission of life. The idea is also present that man's work is God's work and that man needs divine guidance to perform his work properly. This idea is brought out in a prayer composed by a medicine man of the Tharaka Meru of Kenya. The Meru religious outlook is highly theistic and it may be that co-creativity is an element typical of the more theistic systems. In this prayer the supreme being is addressed as *Ngai*.

Ngai, you are the lord,
Help me well,
So that I may get up tomorrow
With my limbs healthy,

And show me the work I have to do.

Ngai, help me that I do not see
Any danger while I work,
Because I know
That there is many a danger.[12]

4 *Judgement*

Seeing that in African Traditional Religion there is no idea
of an historical culmination, or of an eschatological era, it
would be surprising if we found the theme of the Last
Judgement of mankind. On the other hand, it is becoming
increasingly clear that Christian emphasis on judgement as
a 'Last Judgement' betrays a lack of balance. In the Gospel
of St John especially, but even in St Paul and the Synoptics,
the idea is that the judgement of the world has already begun
and that we are being judged here and now. Emphasis on
the hereafter and on the 'last things' is typical of societies in
which there is little commitment to the present life. It is
common in times of persecution, of enslavement and
oppression. In general, the peoples of traditional Africa saw
themselves living a present reality, very much committed to
life in the world, but this did not prevent them from expressing their hope of salvation, nor yet their consciousness
of undergoing a trial in life itself, even a trial that reached
a climax at the moment of death. The supreme being is often
described as a judge, especially where there is a tradition
of sun symbolism connected with him. Like the sun which
travels overhead, or whose 'eye' scans the earth, all things are
open to the supreme being and all secrets are revealed.
Moreover, judgement can be immediate, for sunshine is a
blessing but its heat can be a curse.

Most of the examples of this appear to come from West
Africa, and, certainly, the idea of life being a continuous
learning experience is common to two texts from Nigeria
and Ghana, respectively. In a Yoruba *odu*, or recital, the
hearers are exhorted not 'to run the world hastily' or to act
impatiently.[13] They should be calm and pay due attention
to the future—to the consequence of things. Why? 'On
account of our sleeping.' In other words we must act circum-
spectly because death may catch us unprepared. In an Akan
drum poem from Ghana, the hearer is advised to follow God's

commands.[14] If we are prepared to keep learning from the creator, we shall succeed; we shall be able to lift up the heavens and the earth. For the Ewe of Ghana the judgement at death is explicit.[15] Life is like a hill that one must climb with a load on one's head. The arms are of no use in such a situation; it is the feet that count, and they will be examined for bruises by *Mawu*, the creator who is a searching judge. This judgement takes place at the gates of death, and those who fail the test are punished. The Bushmen of South Africa also apparently expect a judgement 'at the gates of the under-world'[16] in which God will say either 'Come' or 'Go' to those who are brought before him. Those to whom he says 'Come' will remain as his children.

For many African peoples, particularly those for whom mediation is important, the judgement is not so much at the hands of God, the creator, as at the hands of men, the individual's own descendants. If we have no moral worth we shall not be remembered by our posterity, and there will be no offerings. How far the remembrance of the dead is bound up with their immortality is a question that receives different answers from one group to another, but the idea that the dead are affected in some way by human forgetfulness recurs again and again in different societies. Another short, religious poem of the Yoruba of Nigeria exhorts men to behave gently in this life so that they may die peacefully and be blessed with a loving funeral and subsequent funerary offerings.[16] The Ambo of South West Africa (Namibia) express the same sentiment in their religious poetry. The ideal is to 'wait a while' in life, to live long enough for a 'big grave' to be prepared with the right plants and shrubs that will ensure fame and immortality.[17] The lesson once again is that the deeds of this life will shape the attitude of others at one's death. Death must be prepared for in life with calmness and deliberation.

5 The Whole Community

Paul VI in his Letter to Africa of 1967 noted that for the African participation in the life of the community was a precious right and duty for all.[18] Community loyalties are certainly strongly stressed in Africa, and this is reflected in the idiom of everyday speech. For instance, a visitor is soon struck by the frequent use of the first person plural, 'we', 'ours'. Moreover, the gregariousness of Africans manifests itself in countless ways in their patterns of everyday living. This is partly explained by the continued hold, even over urban Africans, of the primary communities of extended family and village. However, even in cases where individuals have been detached from the communities of their homeland, they very often manage to find, or create, a new primary community in the urban areas. This is a surrogate for the extended family or the community of village neighbours, and it may be a church community, or, more often, a circle of colleagues, work-mates, or neighbours belonging to the same ethnic group.

What gives a community loyalty its religious dimension? In certain situations membership of a community may be synonymous with having right on one's side. It may be more or less explicitly believed that one's own group enjoys divine favour, and that others do not. Community membership can become, in these cases, a war of Good versus Evil, represented by one's community on the one hand and the enemies or outsiders on the other. Such ideas are found especially in religious texts—prayers and poems—which deal with warfare and victory. The Kikuyu warriors prayed for victory in supreme confidence that the Creator who had given them a more fertile and more beautiful land than their enemies, had bestowed his favour on them and would empower them to defend this divinely given land.[19] Evans-Pritchard records a Nuer battle hymn with similarly truculent sentiments, exulting in victory over their neighbours the Dinka, and calling down divine vengeance on the British, their Nile steamer, and the people of the Nuba hills.[20]

Happily, the religious dimension of community is ordinarily expressed through more positive and conciliatory sentiments. The community ideal is the maintenance of harmonious relationships, according to pre-determined patterns of structures and roles. Each individual is given his due within the framework of a highly structured society. African traditional societies were strongly communitarian, but that does not mean that they were egalitarian. The structure of the community was given—even divinely given—and the maintenance of the expected social relationships was a religious duty. On the other hand, the sense that the human experience is essentially a shared experience is emphasized in the life-crisis rituals, particularly those at puberty. During such rituals, the initiants are taught to respond to every event as a group, laughing together, crying together, answering together, and performing every activity together. This is not only true of the agricultural peoples, it is equally true of the pastoralists, whose young, warrior age sets, also make a point of acting and reacting in uniformity.

However, this divinely ordered community is not merely a community of the living. Its primary guardians are its deceased members who are still actively involved in its life and development. The ancestors are the creators of society, analogous to the supreme being, the creator of the cosmos. The African community, therefore, is 'the whole community' of living and dead. We have already noted the liaison that is expected to exist between living and dead in the sections on memorial and judgement. In certain societies, like that of the Kikùyu and the Dinka, it is harmony or agreement with the ways of the ancestors that is stressed. In many situations the dead earn their good repute and the religious offerings of their posterity by leading a good life. In fact, the reciprocal relationships that are held to exist between living and dead in so many African societies take on many other forms than these. How far do these relationships have a religious character?

This question was the point at issue in a recent controversy between I. Kopytoff and J. L. Brain.[21] The former argued that ancestors were simply dead elders, who enjoyed a continued social existence, receiving food and drink and other marks of respect and concern as if they were still alive. Michael Singleton has recently argued that ancestors are, for the African, simply symbols for the principle of authority and that filial piety is the experiential basis for ancestor cults.[22] He further argues that, in his own field experience, ancestor shrines and the cults associated with them seem to be disappearing, and he puts this down to the advent of technology and to changes in socio-economic circumstances. His suggestion is that these symbols of authority could and should be replaced by more realistic ones taken from sociology, psychology or—in the Christian context—theology.

My own experience in the field certainly confirms the disappearance of ancestor shrines. I saw only about half a dozen of them in two years, and witnessed prayer taking place at one of them on only one occasion.[23] On the other hand, life was very precarious in that part of western Tanzania, and the demands of a hunting-gathering and shifting cultivating economy, which necessitate frequent moves, make it difficult to rebuild shrine structures in every homestead continually. I found, however, a thousand other outlets among the Kimbu (neighbours of the Konongo among whom Singleton worked) for reciprocity between living and dead. There were elaborate funeral ceremonies, mourning rites, and inheritance or 'second burial' ceremonies focussed on the grave. There were very frequent offerings at graves, and plenty of evidence of this in every burial ground I visited. I witnessed spontaneous first-fruits offerings by huntsmen in the forest, using the minimum of paraphernalia—simply placing a portion of meat in the fork of a tree. I was shown chickens dedicated to the ancestors in many compounds, and I saw child after child wearing the special bead-necklace charm which guarantees ancestral protection. I also witnessed blessing ceremonies in which ancestor-guardians were invoked on departing travellers. I saw portions of food and drink being set aside for the ancestors at the beginning of meals and I saw the reference made to ancestors on numerous social occasions. Impressions I have gained in other parts of the African continent confirm the extreme importance which everywhere attaches to the social celebration of funerals, and to funerary rituals. I have a vivid remembrance of the bus journey from Yaoundé in Caméroun to Libamba, some fifty miles away. Dwellings lined the road through the forest for almost the entire journey, and there was hardly a house that did not have one or more graves in front of it. The graves were mostly of white or painted cement, with crosses, statues and roof structures. Many had plants and flowers growing round them, and a large number had pots, bowls and bottles with offerings of food and drink. One had the impression of driving through an interminable cemetery.

Ancestor veneration may well be symbolic of filial piety and family authority in an authoritarian, kinship-dominated rural society, but it also has to do with personal relationships, with people whom one has known and loved as persons, with respect for the sources of life and human generation. It is also an expression of the religious understanding of life. Not only are ancestors thought to be mediators in formal worship, or even the principal recipients of formal worship, they are intermediaries, divinely given channels of contact with the supreme being or ultimate reality however conceived. The living have a communion of life with them, and they are the guarantors of the stability and progress of the community. Ancestors are credited with more than human powers of knowledge, as Brain pointed out in his rejoinder to Kopytoff. They know the secret thoughts of the living. They know the hidden causes of events as well as their future course. They can possess people and reveal such secrets to them, and they can send sicknesses or misfortunes, as well as cure them or take them away. In every language there is a special vocabulary for referring to ancestors and their activities, quite different from the words which are used when speaking about elders. Death, it seems, makes a difference to the relationships that exist between the living and their deceased elders, but not only death. It is not simply the fact that they are dead that gives the ancestors these powers. As we have already seen, the deceased must have a reputation which gives them power and respect among the living. This reputation is one of having fulfilled the ideals of their society and they are usually— in Christian eyes—ideals which, while they are not opposed to spiritual goals, are nevertheless strongly bound up with concepts of worldly fame and material success. Above all, it is social success which confers immortality and this is inseparable (at least in the traditional, rural kind of community) from kinship and physical generation. Because a man sired children, because he was sought out by innumerable relatives and friends, and because he was rich enough to dispense hospitality and gifts to a large circle of people, he is thought to be equally influential on the other side of the grave. Even if he acquired power through the deployment of unjust force, he may still be an object of cult because of his social influence, although fear, rather than love, may be the dominant sentiment in the worship. There are large numbers of deceased who never become ancestors, children, barren women or sterile men, cripples and social drop-outs, people who die far away from their homeland, outcasts and those who in any way incur social censure or disapproval.

Ancestor veneration is certainly comparable to the Christian cult of saints in so far as it is an expression of the moral ideals of society, and Christian experiments in exploiting African attachment to their ancestors have usually met with success. A recent liturgical experiment is the new Christian funeral rite in Rhodesia, during which, not only are the Christian saints invoked at the graveside and bidden to welcome the departed soul into their company, but the dead man's ancestors are also invoked by name for the same purpose. The new rite has met with widespread approval.

Monica Wilson records a Nyakyusa (Tanzania) text in which a shade (ancestor) is called upon to receive a dead man whose death he has caused.[24] In a later study she records another invocation of the ancestors in which they are accused of complicity in human theft, because they have made food scarce.[25] It is interesting that in the Nyakyusa conception the ancestors are so closely involved in the life of the living, human community that they even share in its guilt. In prayers to the ancestors for the sick, there is a continual insistence on the fact that the sick person and his relatives are their children. This occurs in one prayer text after another in any number of different societies. It is assumed that the ancestors want what is best for their own descendants, and much of prayer is absorbed by the apparent contradiction that those who love them allow them to suffer in spite of this love. This is nothing other than an African approach to the problem of evil so well known to the Old Testament, as well as to the Christian theological tradition. In many cases, the African worshipper is abandoned to the will of the ancestors, even if, like Job, he does not comprehend the situation.[26] In much prayer and ritual addressed to the ancestors there is an easy familiarity, bordering on abruptness or even rudeness. This can be deceptive. Such familiarity is not lacking a real spirit of prayer, but it does emphasize the very close bonds that unite the whole community.

Finally, there is the much discussed element of fear in the veneration of the ancestors. Clearly, fear does play an important part in maintaining the existence of the rituals, and much of the ancestor cult is a belated response to events which are interpreted as vengeance or punishment. It is certainly true that 'perfect love drives out fear',[27] but it is not necessarily true that fear drives out all love. The mental attitude of the African traditional worshipper is not one of unadulterated, craven fear. He believes that his ancestors act justly, that they have a right to punish him and to do what is right in their own eyes. It is this premise of underlying, ancestral love that helps the human sufferer to accept his misfortune. It also accounts for the fact that the most implacable misfortunes are not ascribed to ancestral intervention. It is love, rather than fear, to which the worshipper appeals in the final analysis. 'Why should we be afraid of you?' is the question put by the Acholi to their ancestors,[28] and this question reflects a basic attitude in many other societies. Ancestors are part of the community.

6 Conclusion

There has been no attempt in this chapter to carry out a detailed study of the transformations of a theme across a number of different, African religious systems. What we have tried to do is simply to describe the general character of a universal, life-theme and to propose four examples, at the same time suggesting something of the range of meanings and values that lie behind them in the African religious tradition. We hope also that something of their underlying depth has been revealed—perhaps to the surprise of some Christian readers. If Christians of non-African cultures are surprised at the richness of African religious values, then we must go on to discuss the wider aspects of the dialogue between Christianity and African Traditional Religion, the fundamental problem of communication between different human symbol-systems and value-systems.

Notes

1. Lienhardt, R. G., 1961, *Divinity and Experience*, Oxford.

2. The author has had the experience of giving lecture courses in African religions in six African seminaries of East, Central and Southern Africa. From 1972 to 1974 he was Moderator of the Diploma Examination in Theology of the Department of Religious Studies and Philosophy at Makerere University, Kampala, Uganda.

3. Cf. e.g. Lévi-Strauss, C., 1968, 'The Structural Study of Myth', in *Essays in Social Anthropology*, London, pp. 206-231; and Turner, V., 1969, *The Ritual Process*, London.

4. Sawyerr, H., 1970, *God, Ancestor or Creator?*, London.

5. Paul VI, 1969, 'Closing Discourse to All-Africa Symposium'. *Gaba Pastoral Paper No. 7*, pp. 50-51.

6. Ogot, B. A., 1967, *History of the Southern Luo*, Nairobi.

7. Bernardi, B., 1959, *The Mugwe, A Failing Prophet*, Oxford, p. 202.

8. Kenyatta, J., 1938, *Facing Mount Kenya*, London, p. 247.

9. Lienhardt, R. G., 1961, *Divinity and Experience*, Oxford.

10. *Ibid.*, p. 221.

11. Guillebaud, R., 1950, 'The Idea of God in Ruanda-Urundi', in Smith, E. W. (ed.), *African Ideas of God*, pp. 180-200.

12. Bernardi, *op. cit.*, pp. 124-125.

13. Idowu, E. B., 1962, *Olódùmaré, God in Yoruba Belief*, London, pp. 183-184.

14. Nketia, J. H., 1963, *Drumming in the Akan Communities of Ghana*, London, p. 44.

15. Parrinder, G., 1950, 'The Theistic Beliefs of the Yoruba and Ewe Peoples of West Africa', in Smith, *op cit.*, p. 233.

16. Idowu, *op. cit.*, p. 191.

17. Dymond, G. W., 1950, 'The Ideal of God in Ovamboland, South West Africa', in Smith, *op. cit.*, p. 147.

18. *Africae Terrarum*, no. 12.

19. Kenyatta, J., 1966, *My People of Kikuyu*, Nairobi, pp. 23-24.

20. Evans-Pritchard, E. E. Y., 1956, *Nuer Religion*, Oxford, pp. 46-47.

21. Kopytoff, I., 1971, 'Ancestors as Elders in Africa', *Africa*, XLI, 2, pp. 129-141; Brain, J. L., 1973, 'Ancestors as Elders in Africa: Further Thoughts', in *Africa*, XLIII, 2, pp. 122-133.

22. Singleton, M., 1973, 'On Gas Bottles and Gospels', *African Ecclesiastical Review*, XV, 2, pp. 126-129.

23. The author carried out fieldwork in Ukimbu in South-Western Tanzania from 1964 to 1967. He returned for short visits in 1968, 1969 and 1973.

24. Wilson, M., 1937, *Rituals of Kinship Among the Nyakyusa*, Oxford, p. 70.

25. Wilson M., 1959, *Communal Rituals of the Nyakyusa*, Oxford, p. 77.

26. Cf. Read, M., 1956, *The Ngoni of Nyasaland*, London, p. 198.

27. 1, Jn, iv, 18.

28. Okot p'Bitek, 1971, *The Religion of the Central Luo*, Nairobi, p. 97.

Chapter VIII

Communication between Christian and African Traditional Religious Cultures

1 Overcoming Prejudice

By now it should be obvious that this book is based on the fundamental premise that communication between persons belonging to different cultures is possible. Up to this moment the premise has been assumed, but since many people now query this assumption, it would be as well to consider the question at some length. Doubts arise very often as a result of prejudice, and prejudice itself is an extreme position, in some cases the reaction to another extreme position. An East African poet, James Birihanze, has amusingly sketched some of these attitudes in a poem entitled, 'The Curious Expatriate'. In this excerpt the expatriate is speaking.

> My father was a D.C.[1]
> In Karamoja before *Yuhuru*.[2]
> He told me Africans were unlike us,
> That it was impossible
> To understand them.
> He felt sure they did not defaecate,
> Else why had they no latrines?
> Why should they quarrel
> And fight over their cattle?
> I want to prove he was wrong.
> There is a reason for everything,
> And I must find out
> What makes them tick.[3]

It is an ancient prejudice of the white administrator or missionary that: 'Africans are unlike us' or that 'It is impossible to understand them'. What the white man was saying in most cases was: 'African behaviour is not meaningful to me, therefore it is probably not meaningful in itself.' Such an attitude is about the most effective block to communication that can exist. It is the reflection of an ethnocentrism that refuses to make the effort to understand others except on one's own terms. Another extreme position is that of the administrator's son. This young man has grown up in the era of the human sciences, of psychology and sociology which teach that nothing ever happens by accident. 'There is a reason for everything.' This represents a complete swing of the pendulum, the affirmation that all human behaviour, however bizarre, can be understood and interpreted according to the yardstick of scientific rationality. No doubt, the poet was not belittling the achievements of social science, but he was definitely exhibiting some scepticism about the claims made on behalf of cultural translation, about the objectivity of western scientific method and about the westerner's pre-occupation with details, *minutiae* and *trivia*.

The poet was also exhibiting an amused annoyance at the army of white researchers, so intent on collecting their African specimens that they forget the African also has a point of view, and that a human encounter should take place. This is the new form of colonialism—a scientific colonialism, as basically ethnocentric as the attitude of the old administrator. It is fortunate that the poet is only amused. Many Africans—even among the educated classes—are filled with revulsion. They are sick and tired of being put in a show-case, of being analysed from every angle by foreigners who look for latent functions and hidden motivations, but who do not really share their lives or their loves. When will the African speak about himself? To whom will he speak about himself? Does he have to speak at all—or is this just a white fad, this study of other people's cultures? If he speaks, is he merely pandering to the curiosity of the 'curious expatriate'? For Africans—and indeed, for anyone else who thinks twice about it—it is more important to live life than to study it.

These are the questions that lie behind the prejudices and extreme reactions on the part of the African élite. One attitude is that of Okot p'Bitek, that Africa must throw over-board all the achievements of expatriates in the field of African studies. That Africans must start again from scratch. A related attitude is simply a revival of the prejudice of the white, colonial administrator, that expatriates cannot understand Africans, and that the only studies of Africa which are valid are those carried out by Africans themselves. This attitude is based now upon African ethnocentrism, rather than upon western ethnocentrism. A good case can be made out, I think, for a moratorium on studies by white scholars, to give Africans the chance to exploit the obvious advantages they enjoy in the study of their own cultures, but it would not be wise to accede to a complete close-down, either because there are, as yet, insufficient African scholars, or because a body of opinion exists that it is wiser to be silent than to speak. Silence about the cultural heritage of Africa will do no one any good, nor is it a human attitude. Human nature requires that we speak about what we know, that we communicate our experience. The commonsense approach is to put to maximum use the information already accumulated as well as the talents and opportunities of available African scholars, while at the same time, trying to encourage more African academics to enter the field.

On one important point Africans are very right indeed. It is more important to live life than to study it, or rather, it is useless to study the life of a society without sharing in it. We shall come back to this consideration later in this chapter, but we can say right from the beginning that communication between human cultures can only take place effectively through dialogue and participation, through listening and through readiness to learn. This means not only that westerners must listen to Africans, but also that Africans should not abandon western ideas and methods. These are channels of communication which must not be blocked. Both interlocutors must make the effort to enter into the mind of the other. Talk of 'Black Theology' or 'African Theology' is excellent, but it must mean a contribution to other theologies. If it is meant to be exclusive, then it ceases to be theology. No single culture has a monopoly of God, just as no single culture has a monopoly of human experience.

2 The Problem of Objective, 'Scientific' Criteria

A subject for debate among sociologists and social anthropologists has been the extent to which the social sciences are 'sciences'. Are these disciplines sciences in the same way that the physical sciences are sciences? Can they achieve the same degree of certainty? Can they make universal laws and predictions? Many social anthropologists would argue that the study of human societies is not a science but a humanity, and being the study of man in his social aspect, pre-eminent among the humanities. They would not, however, go further and say that a humanity is incapable of any certainty whatsoever. Like the historian, for example, the social scientist believes that his discipline is rational, and that he presents human behaviour and human ideas in a way that satisfies certain criteria of objectivity and rationality. Human modes of thought differ one from another, and in presenting to people a mode of thought which differs from their own, one is confronted with the ineluctable fact that translation is ultimately impossible. Western scientific thinking claims a completely objective knowledge of reality, uninfluenced by cultural suppositions, and this claim went unchallenged until the second half of the 20th century. Anthropologists, in particular, never questioned it. It was assumed that, even if cultural translation was always cultural treason, differences between one mode of thinking and another were checkable according to objective facts, and it was, of course, found that many, if not most, differences derived from an unscientific attitude on the part of non-western thought-systems. Many of their ideas simply did not accord with the objective facts as westerners knew them.

Without wishing to accuse non-westerners of an inability to reason or of differences in their biological and psychological make-up as human beings, Lucien Lévy-Bruhl used the unpleasant and misleading word 'pre-logical' to refer to the unscientific and uncritical categories of thought which typify non-western societies. According to Lévy-Bruhl, what characterizes the 'pre-logical' mentality is the inability of people in some cultures to perceive the contradictions that exist between their own ideas and objective reality. For Lévy-Bruhl, therefore, there are two types of mentality, the 'scientific' and the 'pre-logical'. At the present time of writing, it is more than thirty years since Lévy-Bruhl put forward these views, and no one shares them today. Nobody, for example, believes that a large proportion of the human race is socially conditioned to the extent that they are unable to perceive contradictions between ideas and objective reality. However, anthropologists have accepted, and continue to accept, that there are contradictions, and have made it their

133

concern to demonstrate to their readers how a system of thinking can maintain itself in spite of obvious objections. They have shown, for example, that members of these societies subscribe to closed, if logical, systems of thought and that they are uninterested in testing their ideas and beliefs scientifically. While they are perfectly capable of empirical thinking in certain situations, in others the problem of a contradiction simply does not arise. The classic example of this explanation is that of Evans-Pritchard's masterly study of the Azande of Sudan, first published in 1937.[4] It was not until the late 1950s and 1960s that Peter Winch challenged it, to be followed in the seventies by Horton and others.[5]

Although Evans-Pritchard did not hold that Europeans think more logically than Azande, he did believe that they think more scientifically—that their culture disposes them to hold ideas which are more often in accord with objective reality. It was Winch who demonstrated that the concept of 'objective reality' has no intelligibility outside the context of scientific thinking. In other words, notions such as 'objective reality' are culture-bound, and, in saying that African thinking is not conformed to objective reality, one is simply saying that human societies have different concepts of reality, and that the thoughts of one society do not necessarily correspond to the idea of reality in another society. In fact, one has no right to expect that they should correspond. Winch, rightly, goes even further than this, and points out that there are different levels of reality within a single culture, referring to different uses of language. All languages distinguish between the real and the unreal, but this is not to say that the statements: 'God is real' and 'this tree is real' are using the word 'real' in precisely the same way. Clearly, they are not, and it is no use whatever employing empirical tests to try and discover the reality of God. This is not, of course, to say that human beings do not either make mistakes or misuse language. They do. What it says is that ideas and beliefs common to members of different societies cannot simply be written off because they do not accord with one particular society's idea of reality at one particular level.

Evans-Pritchard's fundamental worry (and this he expressed to me personally at the time of the debate with Winch[6]) was the threat of relativism. Is the logical outcome of Winch's objection the conclusion that other cultures are not only untranslatable but even unknowable? If so, the social sciences and, indeed, all inter-cultural dialogue, all missionary work, and the idea of a Catholic or Universal Church, fall to the ground. Communication between human beings is impossible. Before trying to answer this question and restoring faith in human communication, it would be worthwhile going a little further into the question of science and its relevance for an understanding of reality.

3 Science and Symbol

If human cultures cannot be compared and contrasted in accordance with a concept of objective reality common to all language levels in each of the thought-systems, what becomes of the bed-rock of physical science itself—the touchstone, as anthropologists and sociologists have imagined, of objective certainty? And what becomes of the assumption that the western world thinks scientifically, whereas other cultures, by choice, place the emphasis on imagery and symbolism? The answer is that this whole edifice of western scientific certainty has been blown sky high, and that the hand that lobbed the bombshell is Thomas Kuhn. In his *The Structure of Scientific Revolutions*, published in 1970,[7] Kuhn shows how scientists obtain their most effective achievements through the application of a paradigm or pattern of images. Using images and symbols such as 'fields', 'waves', 'atoms' and so forth, they interpret the behaviour of the natural world. The paradigm is 'open-ended' in that it is a developing phenomenon dependent upon continuing research and repeated application. Eventually, as Kuhn shows, the paradigm becomes worn out. Exceptions multiply, and research becomes preoccupied with a set of anomalies that cannot be disregarded. The time then comes when the original paradigm is replaced by a new one. Scientists become attached to their paradigms with all the fervour of a religious believer, and the reigning paradigm can never be challenged or called in question. It never occurs to anyone to do so, for to challenge the current paradigm is to rob the scientist of his very element —the very conditions of scientific thought and progress.

After Kuhn it is no longer possible to draw a clear distinction between scientific and symbolical thought, because science itself turns out to be no more than a pattern of images as symbolical as any African or other non-western mode of thought. All human communication and all human thought-systems are essentially symbolical, and each system has its own choice and arrangement of symbols. However, there are certain aspects of scientific research which distinguish it from other forms of symbolical thinking and which render it significant for human communication. One of these aspects is the open-endedness already referred to. Scientific thinking is not static; it is an invitation to search and explore the natural world, using the favoured paradigm as a torch to cast light on everything which surrounds us. It is precisely because of this dynamism that the paradigm runs the risk of becoming exhausted and of being replaced by another.

Another significant aspect is the acceptance of pluralism. The scientist not only is forced ultimately to abandon one paradigm for another when the time comes, but he readily accepts the fact of specialization. The natural world is carved up into different sectors, illumined from different angles simultaneously by different paradigms, not all of them easy to reconcile with one another. The scientist accepts the validity of these different approaches. Not only does he also accept the possibility of a single man, understanding and using several paradigms at different moments, but he is even able to borrow ideas and images from one paradigm and introduce them into another, thus forging links between different branches of scientific knowledge.

We can now appreciate that scientific disciplines can help us to achieve a mutual understanding of human cultures. This they do, not because they measure them all against objective standards of reality which are culture-free, but because they provide a point of entry into several cultures at the same time. The paradigms elaborated by sociologists and anthropologists, using images such as 'social organism', 'social structure' and so on, shed a certain light on the different systems of ideas and behaviour. They cannot illuminate everything, and the more rigorously they are applied in unending research, the more anomalies and obscurities are revealed. Very far from everything in a given culture is susceptible of translation into the imagery of the sociological paradigm, but the effort to apply the paradigm brings the scientist into contact with another mode of thinking. Being essentially open and disposed to pluralism, the scientific approach to the study of human cultures favours,

136

if it cannot satisfactorily articulate, the simultaneous experiencing of several cultures, and, as happens in interdisciplinary studies, cross-fertilization can, and does take place.

4 The Sharing of Experience

It is through symbols that cultures and languages give expression to human experience. Scientific language in particular, even though it is 'contaminated' by western culture, does help to canalize, organize and develop human experience of the natural world. However, when all is said and done, we are confronted by a multitude of differing symbol systems, all struggling to give expression to human experience. Human experiences also differ, in response to differing sociocultural stimuli and conditioning, yet human life necessarily involves certain fundamental notions that impose limits on these differences. Among these fundamental notions are the very life processes themselves, birth, death, procreation, eating, drinking, etc., as well as friendship, alienation and other concomitants of a life that is essentially shared. Expressed in various ways, according to differing cultural patterns, these are elements of universal, human experience, which in the last chapter we referred to as 'life themes'.

At the level of such fundamental notions as life themes, it is clear that talk of a cross-cultural sharing of experience is perfectly meaningful. Even at the level of culturally conditioning human experiences, it is possible to some extent for a member of a given culture to be conditioned, and to respond to experiences according to the dictates of a second culture. As a result, the two ways of experiencing and expressing experience become part of his make-up, and he may come to appreciate that certain experiences and symbols are preferable to other experiences and symbols. Like the bilingual man, he discovers that when speaking one language, a word from his second language better expresses a particular experience, or he may simply enjoy the luxury of possessing an alternative set of images.

It is essential that the interlocutors in the dialogue between different religious traditions become culturally bilingual. To some extent they must be capable of experiencing two religious cultures at the same time. The Christian must have a genuine experience of African religion, but he must experience it as a Christian. For his part, the African Traditional Religionist must experience Christianity from within his own tradition. Such cultural bilingualism must be truly scientific, that is to say open-ended. It must act as a stimulus to further discovery and to the sharing and inter-play of symbols from the two systems.

We have said that all human cultures have concepts of the real and the unreal and that all cultures have criteria of logic. Are there also universal criteria of truth? Obviously there are. A people must believe that its ideas correspond or do not correspond to an independent reality, even if the understanding of reality varies and changes in space and time. The understanding of reality is dependent to some extent on different contexts, and it can be (as it is in the Western world) a developing or changing understanding. Nevertheless, if there were no universal criteria of truth, people would be incapable of expressing their ideas and beliefs in languages and systems of symbols, and it would be impossible to have any scientific knowledge about such languages and symbol systems. It is precisely because there are universal criteria of truth and logic that a man can become bilingual, that he can enter a culture that is not his own by birth and upbringing. However, human beings are capable of untruth and of resistance to the truth. Consciously or unconsciously they may adhere to ideas and beliefs which run counter to their criteria of truth and this can be demonstrated.

It might be argued that all of this makes truth and falsity into something subjective, and that the ultimate, critical synthesis of the insights of different cultures is the task of an individual, relying exclusively on his own experience. However, this is not so. We are dealing with a social understanding of reality, with collective expressions of experiences which are shared. It is, of course, possible for an individual to miss the point or meaning of a particular expression, or for his experience to be rendered untypical as a result of subjective factors. The only safeguard against such eventualities is for a number of interlocutors to engage in the dialogue from both sides. This is not a task for one or two isolated specialists, but a common task for us all. In the pluralistic world of the end of the 20th century all of us have the vocation to become culturally bilingual. Without communication between cultures and religions it is impossible for any to survive, and it is especially difficult for a universal religion like Christianity to survive.

5 Cultural Pluralism and the Universal Church

'Society' is the name that we give to the actions, interactions and relationships that exist between human beings in so far as we can form a mental picture of them. Some of these relationships are 'grid' relationships or relationships that constitute a network centred on the individual. Other relationships are group relationships, or relationships that exist between individuals because they all belong to a group like a family or a village community. Among groups there are varying degrees of involvement and intimacy. Some are 'primary', like the family, absorbing the whole man; others are 'secondary' involving only a segment of man's life, for example a political party, or a trade union.

Social relationships take on enduring shapes involving large numbers of individuals in space and time and being transmitted from generation to generation and from group to group. For the sociologist or social anthropologist these social facts have patterns or structures, as they call them, which operate in the minds of the members of society and which can be observed and tested experimentally by the social scientist. An ordinary human society has many overlapping structures, family structure, political structure, structure of religious belief, structure of morality and so forth. These structures are related to the physical environment which offers a limited number of—not necessarily contradictory—choices to help solve its basic material problems of living, food, clothing, housing. The way a society chooses, arranges and modifies the material things offered by its physical environment is called its economy, and a society must adapt its social institutions and organization, its patterns of settlement and movement, to its chosen economy, as well as to its continuing tradition of choices and adaptations.

It is in this way that a human society creates its own way of life or 'culture' and that its members learn and teach their culture in succeeding generations. All the learned aspects of human ideas and behaviour are what we call 'culture', and culture is made up of social facts, economic facts, techniques and everything else that an individual learns as a member of his society. Especially important is the area of ultimate concern that we term 'religion' and which integrates the view which a society has of man, his place in the universe and his destiny. Pre-colonial Africa saw multiple adaptations to differing environments, as well as a relative isolation and relative interaction among them. This socio-economic recipe produced the tribal cultures of Africa, each with their own language, social organization, religion and world view.

The social scientist knows that societies are not static things. To live is to change, and all societies and cultures are continually changing. Even social structures are not unchanging, harmonious systems; they sometimes exhibit discord and tension. Structures are themselves a developing process. In all social change there are both continuities and discontinuities; nor is social change a uniform process. Finally, social change is neither uncontrollable nor irresistible; individuals can initiate change and resist change at different cultural levels. There are two main kinds of social change: regular change and structural change. Regular change operates in a homogeneous or unitary society where emphasis is on the primary group, and it allows for shifts in the balance of forces within society, for the release of tensions, and for processes of reconciliation. Structural change, on the other hand, creates new institutions and systems of ideas, often as a result of external forces influencing and supporting potential innovators in the society in question.

One type of structural change, which is sometimes called organizational change, brings a new kind of society into existence. It happens when not only structures are changed but the very scale of social relationships is enlarged. When this happens, society is no longer unitary and homogeneous. It becomes a pluralistic society, possessing not only a plurality of groupings, but a plurality of cultures, of value-systems and beliefs. In this type of society the secondary group takes on a necessary importance; individuals are confronted with alternatives and contradictions; many situations are transient because of the rapidity of change; and superficial, functional relationships between people are multiplied. By and large, this is the kind of change which the world today, including Africa, is experiencing.

Not all the consequences of this type of change are negative; there are also positive and constructive factors. One of these is the growth of inter-dependence between different groups or communities, each helping to supply each other's needs, material, social or moral. Another consequence is the process known as incorporation. This is a term which refers to the degree of mutual influence which different groups and different systems of values have on one another in the pluralistic society. Finally there is the factor known as congruence of values, according to which a certain overlapping or convergence between these different systems takes place.

It is important to understand that this type of social change is not merely the exchange of one unitary for another unitary society, of, for example, a traditional African society for a European society. What emerges as a result of this kind of change is a new type of society altogether. A radical transformation takes place, albeit with some elements of continuity. The Christian, faced with the emergence of the pluralistic society, has three basic options. The first option is simply one of passivity or drift. The Christian refuses to become involved or to exercise any control or selectivity in the process of change. Change becomes the master, and the result is disorientation, relativism, superficiality and ultimately de-humanization. As a value-system in this new kind of society, the Church, under this option, will simply disintegrate, lacking purpose or relevance.

The second option is to attempt to put the clock back and recreate the unitary type of society. Many Church leaders hanker after the old homogeneous Church, proclaiming a single, undifferentiated message for all to accept or reject. The basic idea is to get people to transfer their allegiance from other groups to the Church-group, in other words, conversion. The problem is that in a pluralistic society wholesale transfers of religious allegiance are unlikely to take place. It is only through such processes as have been described, interdependence, incorporation and congruence, that conversions can take place. A Church which cuts itself off from these processes becomes irrelevant in a pluralistic society. In the language of sociology it becomes 'privatist' or 'particularist', and in the language of popular idiom it 'drops out'.

The third option does not reject the idea of conversions. On the contrary, the transfer of religious allegiance continues and is sought after. However, religious allegiance is more sophisticated, and the primary or informal religious group to which the individual adheres in the first instance becomes a means of incorporation in the pluralistic society. It is of absolute importance that Christians rediscover the primary group in this changing situation—not as a means of isolation but as a means of incorporation. The activity which characterizes the third option is above all religious dialogue—dialogue between churches, religions and religion-based cultures. The fruits of dialogue for the Christian include a better self-identification. This comes about through a more sophisticated understanding of Scripture and Theology and through a conscious narrowing of the gap between official and popular Christianity. Another consequence of religious dialogue would be the hoped-for convergence or growth towards a common horizon of truth. In fact, the processes of organizational change correspond exactly with the major consequences of religious dialogue. Interdependence, or the experience of serving groups with different outlooks and religious needs, makes a church aware of the differences which divide religious believers. Incorporation implies the experience of learning new interests from other communities, while congruence of values means the enlarging of the area of agreement.

It is clear that in a pluralistic world a homogeneous religious system that is trying to swallow up other systems is out of place. What is required is a differentiated system which is in real contact through religious dialogue with other systems of beliefs and values in the various localities. A universal church, therefore, must be prepared to admit cultural pluralism. The question is: Can Christianity admit such pluralism without ceasing to be universal? Are unity and diversity compatible? The answer to this question depends on how sophisticated an understanding of Christianity one has. If one believes in an exclusive 'holier-than-thou' church-community which has a monopoly of truth and salvation, dispensing these to all who would submit to her jurisdiction, then the answer to our two questions is obviously 'No'. If, on the other hand, one believes in the cosmic Christ, loving, saving and guiding men of goodwill, even though they are ignorant of his name and mission, the answer could be 'Yes'.

If it is true that human societies and cultures share fundamental notions about truth and reason, and that they are all preoccupied with certain fundamental themes of life, the

Christian must go even further, believing that Christ, who as God-Man, is the summit of humanity, lives at the heart of all this human experience. The Christian Church has to proclaim Christ and his Gospel, but before doing so, she must listen obediently to him. Where does the Church hear Christ's voice? The listening Church hears him first of all in Scripture, the historic Christ, speaking through the Biblical cultures among which he lived and in which his coming was foretold and remembered. However, in the second place, the listening Church hears the voice of the same Christ in human, socio-cultural situations. Christ is no longer bound by the limits of a single, human life-time, lived in a particular culture or set of cultures. He is the Risen Christ, the Everlasting and Universal Man, whom we meet today in our human communities and whom it is the Church's duty, in the light of Scripture, to point out and acknowledge.

The universal vocation of Christianity is enhanced, rather than diminished, by the experience of cultural pluralism. In the mutual experiencing of Christ in differing cultures, there is an enrichment of the kind we referred to as 'cultural bilingualism'. There is also an accumulation of insights, as Christians in contact with differing cultures influence one another at the universal level. Finally, there is a prospect of a unity which is coming into being, the hope that in sharing an experience of one another's cultures a growing convergence is being promoted. Truth is ultimately a horizon towards which we are moving, rather than a precious possession which we already have, and which we are already able to parcel out.

Words like these are fine-sounding, but a great deal must be worked out in practice. What are the pastoral implications, for example, of these ideas for Christians in Africa? What shapes must religious dialogue take there? Equally important: How does all this affect the genesis of an African Christian Theology, as one expression of a differentiated Christianity in a pluralistic and changing world? In the final chapter we shall try to deal with some of these questions.

Notes

1. District Commissioner.
2. Political Independence. Karamoja is a district in north-eastern Uganda.
3. James N. Birihanze, 'The Curious Expatriate', in *Ghala (East Africa Journal)*, Vol. viii, no. 7, July 1971, p. 35.
4. Evans-Pritchard, E. E. Y., 1937, *Witchcraft, Oracles and Magic Among the Azande*, Oxford.
5. Cf. Winch, P., 1967, 'Understanding a Primitive Society', in Phillips, D. Z. (ed.), *Religion and Understanding*, Oxford, pp. 9-62; and Horton, R., and Finnegan, R. (eds), *Modes of Thought*, London.
6. Personal comment after attending a debate at the Commonwealth Institute, Oxford, between Peter Winch and Alisdair McIntyre, February 12th, 1964.
7. Kuhn, T. S., 1970, *The Structure of Scientific Revolutions*, Chicago.

Chapter IX

Adaptation or Incarnation?

1 A Christian Ministry of Dialogue in Africa

During 1974, in the month of August, the Vatican Secretariat for Non-Christian Religions organized a consultation on African Traditional Religion at Gaba Pastoral Institute, Kampala. This meeting was the first of its kind anywhere in English-speaking Africa. Until 1974 the Roman Catholic Church had never given any official recognition to the religious traditions of Africa as worthy partners in dialogue, on a par with the world religions of Asia and the Near East. At this meeting about twenty Roman Catholic participants, representing the seven countries of Kenya, Malawi, Rhodesia, South Africa, Tanzania, Uganda and Zambia, as well as the Vatican Secretariat itself, met local experts in African religion and local religious specialists.

From the reports of the participants at this meeting it soon became clear that the Roman Catholic Church in these English-speaking African countries was everywhere fraught with tensions on the subject of Non-Christian religion. At every level in the Church were found people whose attitude to African Traditional Religion was wholly negative. They accepted unreservedly the initial rejection of African religion by the first generation of missionaries. For many it was questionable whether the name 'religion' could even be given to the beliefs and practices of 'pagans', and the latter were commonly despised as having no religion. In some cases, inaccurate generalizations made by the first missionaries had been adopted and were still in use, such as the use of the slanderous word 'witchcraft' to refer to traditional religious practices. These people also possessed a very static view of the Christian Church. Everything that was the teaching and practice of the first missionaries in the late nineteenth century was of equal importance. The playing of harmoniums, for example, was as integral a part of the Christian faith as the real presence in the Eucharist. Such people had a real fear of 'paganism' and they looked upon current moves to Africanize the life and worship of the Church as a betrayal, calculated to produce what they termed a 'half-caste Christianity'.

Another tension was that of the educated man, particularly the young academic, strongly committed to cultural independence, who is scandalized by the apparent imperviousness of the Church to African culture. His resentment at missionary iconoclasm is bitter in the extreme and he is tempted to reject Christianity altogether. Finally there is the tension, already alluded to in the first chapter, of an inner duality in the make-up of the vast majority of ordinary Christians, pulled in both directions at once and puzzled by recent trends towards African culture in a Church which they had supposed was unreservedly hostile to it. The general picture in the Church was one of lack of guidance or stimulation from above. At the official level there was little or no support for dialogue with African Traditional Religion. On the contrary, there was considerable hostility to it. Any initiatives taken were purely local and were the responsibility, for the most part, of private individuals who often ran the risk of disapproval, if not actual victimization. All of this represents a potentially dangerous, divisive situation. If the Church is not to fall apart, there must be an attempt at reconciliation between these different sections of people, and a reconciliation can only occur as a consequence of general re-education in accordance with the trends of contemporary theology and pastoral practice.

In spite of the very general fear of 'paganism', the Roman Catholic Church in these English-speaking countries of Africa is already beginning to pay lip-service to the concept of cultural pluralism. There is considerable talk about 'Adaptation' and 'Africanization'. In practice, this has meant, in the years following the Second Vatican Council, the production of vernacular liturgical texts and the creation of local musical settings for these texts. Very little has been done to grapple with traditional religious ideas, or to create an African Philosophy and Theology. Still less, has there been any concern to create typically African Church structures. Finally, far too little has been achieved in the realm of the plastic arts, painting, sculpture, architecture and design. In the catechetical field, some new religious education courses have been created that have seriously attempted to utilize the riches of traditional religion and culture.[1] However, these are unfortunately offset by a stream of catechetical publications that continue to use opprobrious terms in connection with African Traditional Religion and inspire a mistrust and contempt for it.

The meeting of the Secretariat for Non-Christian Religions at Gaba strongly affirmed its belief in the real possibility of religious dialogue between Christians and the religious traditions of Africa and saw this dialogue as both desirable and necessary. It was made very clear by the spokesmen for African Traditional Religion who attended the meeting, that dialogue with Christians was strongly desired by themselves also. The participants felt too that there was a danger of pragmatism in fostering African adaptation in the Church, without at the same time encouraging serious and systematic study of African religion and culture, through participation, observation and genuine dialogue.

An objection which the Gaba meeting felt that it had to answer was the pessimistic assertion that interlocutors for a dialogue with African Traditional Religion simply do not exist, and that there simply are no real spokesmen for the African side. It was felt that if Christians thought dialogue was necessary the onus lay on them to find the interlocutors. They, therefore, went on to identify the possible interlocutors. In the first place it was thought that spokesmen for an authentic and living religious tradition still existed and that there are still priests, shrine-keepers, spirit-mediums, diviners, doctors and other religious specialists available for dialogue. In the second place there are representatives of modern religious movements that are more or less neo-traditional. In the case of African Independent Churches, the origin of many of them was due to a failure in dialogue. Institution of dialogue will do everyone a service. Then there are the ordinary Christians with their unresolved duality, who are in need of internal dialogue to help them integrate the different outlooks, or at least to confront them consciously. More sophisticated people require a situational theology, answering to their own, real needs, but even these people have to come to terms with submerged traditional values at one stage or another. Finally, came the very interesting suggestion that great religious personalities of the past are really interlocutors in one way or another. Their memory is often well documented in oral tradition and cherished by people living today. The example of Kintu in Uganda has already been mentioned in Chapter Seven. It is possible to enter into dialogue with a living tradition that goes back to these religious personalities.

There is here a very large programme waiting to be carried out, but the question is: How are we to make a start? Who will make a start? A first suggestion came from Fr Alexander Chima, representing Malawi. This was the idea of setting up a ministry of dialogue. The meeting did not spell out in any detail what this ministry might entail, and this might be a useful thing to do here. One thing it did stipulate and that was that such a ministry should enjoy official approval. Perhaps what is needed is not any elaborate structure at national or international level, but rather a team of people in each country responsible for mobilizing others at all levels. It could initiate local projects of research and contact with religious traditions. For this work the team members would have to be adequately trained in social anthropology, the study of religions, and methods of fieldwork. They could also meet clergy, religious and teachers in the local churches and help them to develop a more tolerant and discerning attitude towards African Traditional Religion, as well as try to vet catechetical literature and remove offensive terms and statements.

Another area of updating which such a team could cover would be in the seminaries and universities. In the seminaries it is essential that those training for the ministry should be favourably disposed towards religious dialogue with Non-Christian religions, through lectures and discussions, as well as through fieldwork projects during the vacations. In the universities the team could contribute through lectures, and through participation in conferences and seminars to the removal of prejudice and ignorance in academic circles. They would try to straddle the gulf that lies between the university and the church, introducing science and system into church programmes of research and dialogue, and dispelling academic ignorance of Christian aims and methods. Finally, the team would be on hand to offer advice, based on their own research and experience, to those committees charged with catechetical and liturgical renewal in the country. The creation of such a team is not a luxury. Given the tensions and contradictions of the present situation, it is a strict necessity to have such a ministry of dialogue and to heed the advice of the Secretariat for Non-Christian Religions on this point. In the next section of this chapter we shall see that such a ministry has a role to play also in the process of theological 'incarnation'.

2 The Demand for an Incarnational Theology

We have already quoted the opinion of Bishop Sastre that adaptation implies the elevation of the particular to the universal,[2] and in all discussion of African Theology the question of the universal level is of the utmost importance. In 1968, Professor Vanneste contributed a paper on the topic: 'Universal Theology and African Theology' to the Fourth Theological Week at Lovanium University, Kinshasa. His conclusion began as follows:

> I very willingly admit that in insisting continually on the fact that all theology must aim at universality to be true, I have been led to underline the unity, rather than the plurality, of theological science. However, it is, perhaps, not entirely unjust to reproach the partisans of unity of having a concept that is above all that of a western unity.[3]

He then goes on to say that it is not our differences that should be stressed, but rather the fact that different cultures and traditions are all of them making their contribution to a universal theology that is more universal or Catholic. It is right that the unity of Christian Theology should be stressed, but it is equally right that universal theology should not be presented as the translation into many languages of a theology evolved wholly within a particular cultural tradition. This is to reduce the churches of the non-western world to a state of passivity and perpetual juniority that is completely inconsistent with the idea of a universal church, and it is, as Professor Vanneste rightly says, to equate theological unity with a unity imposed by the western world. To be entirely honest, this is the concept of theological unity which has reigned up until the Second Vatican Council. It is the concept of theological unity expressed by the term 'adaptation'. The idea which this term suggests is one of the western missionary announcing the Gospel in the terms of his own culture, and of the young, mission church adapting this message to suit local idiosyncrasies. The word 'adaptation' cannot help but convey an activity that is peripheral, non-essential—even superficial. At first, the concept of 'adaptation' was hailed on all sides, by African Christians as well as by missionaries. Even though it was not seen as committing the Church to religious dialogue with African tradition, and perhaps because of this, adaptation, as the means by which the African Church could develop its own life-style, was highly welcome. It was only slowly realized that the concept of adaptation contained within itself the seeds of perpetual western superiority and domination. The reaction has been quite violent.

At the Roman Synod of 1974, the theme of which was 'Evangelization', the Bishops of Africa repudiated 'the theology of adaptation' in no uncertain terms and opted for what they called 'the theology of incarnation'. The relevant section of their declaration reads as follows:

Our theological thinking must remain faithful to the authentic tradition of the Church and, at the same time, be attentive to the life of our communities and respectful of our traditions and languages, that is of our philosophy of life.

Following this idea of mission, the Bishops of Africa and Madagascar consider as being completely out-of-date, the so-called theology of adaptation. In its stead, they adopt the theology of incarnation. The young churches of Africa and Madagascar cannot refuse to face up to this basic demand. They accept the fact of theological pluralism within the unity of faith, and consequently they must encourage, by all means, African theological research. Theology must be open to the aspiration of the people of Africa, if it is to help Christianity to become incarnate in the life of the peoples of the African Continent. To achieve this, the young Churches of Africa and Madagascar must take over more and more responsibility for their own evangelization and total development. They must combine creativity with dynamic responsibility.

It is important to note here that this way of ours must strengthen the bonds of unity within the universal Church, and in the first place with the Apostolic See. The grave problems of the hour and the very nature of the Church itself, the Body of Christ, make this imperative.[4]

For the Bishops of Africa and Madagascar in 1974 the theology of adaptation is completely out-of-date. The accent is on the creativity and dynamic responsibility of the local church while remaining faithful to the authentic, universal tradition and to the bonds of unity within the universal Church. Christianity is to become 'incarnate' in the life of the peoples of Africa. Beyond saying this, the notion of an incarnational theology, interesting as it is, is not sufficiently spelt out, and a synodal declaration is, perhaps, hardly the place to do this.

However, it was precisely because the accent on pluralism might give rise to misunderstanding, that the Pope was led, in the self-same Synod, to go to the other extreme in stressing theological unity. In his Address at the conclusion of the Synod, six days after the publication of the African Bishops' Declaration, Pope Paul VI had this to say:

> We sincerely rejoice at the increasing vitality of the particular Churches and of their ever more manifest will to assume all their proper responsibilities. At the same time we hope that proportionate care will be taken so that, in the furthering of this essential aspect of ecclesial reality, no harm will come to the firmness of the *communio* with the other particular Churches and with the Successor of Saint Peter, to whom the Lord has entrusted the serious and enduring role—one full of love—of tending his lambs and sheep (Jn. 21, 13-17), of confirming his brethren, (Lk. 22, 32) and of being the foundation and sign of the unity of the Church (Mt. 16, 18-20).[5]

After quoting the Vatican Council Document on the Church (*Lumen Gentium* 22) on the subject of the 'full, supreme, and universal power' of the Pope—itself an echo of Canon 218 which contains the same trio of adjectives—Paul VI goes on to touch the subject of theology in particular:

> Thus we consider necessary a word on the need of find-

ing a better expression of faith to correspond to the racial, social and cultural milieux. This is indeed a necessary requirement of authenticity and effectiveness of Evangelization; it would nevertheless be dangerous to speak of diversified theologies according to continents and cultures. The content of the faith is either Catholic or it is not. All of us on the other hand have received the faith of a constant tradition: Peter and Paul did not transform it to adapt it to the Jewish, Greek or Roman world; but they watched vigilantly over its authenticity and over the truth of its single message presented in a diversity of languages. (Ac. 2, 8.)[6]

At first sight, the Pope's comments look like a douche of cold water on everything that was said on the subject by the Bishops of Africa and Madagascar. However, further reflection produces the conviction that this is not so. Quite apart from the unlikelihood of the Pope engaging in an open battle with the episcopate of an entire continent on the floor of the Synod Hall, it is clear that, although both statements make opposite emphases, they do not, in fact, contradict one another. The African Bishops 'accept the fact of theological pluralism'. The Pope warns of the danger in speaking about 'diversified theologies according to continents and cultures', and declares that 'the content of the faith is either Catholic (universal) or it is not'.

The distinction between pluralism and diversity is important. Pluralism is not a mere diversity, but diversity-in-unity. Error and enmity produce the wrong kind of diversity, scattering people and keeping them apart. Pluralism, on the other hand, signifies, in this context, that many elements are brought together in unity. In fact, talk of unity presupposes pluralism, since it would otherwise have no meaning. Unity of what? Diversity-in-unity suggests a richness, an organized unity, patterned on the organic unity of the Trinity itself. This type of diversity-in-unity was very beautifully described by Pope Paul VI himself ten years earlier. The occasion was the historic meeting with the Bishops of the Oriental Rites in the Church of the White Fathers in Jerusalem. On that occasion the Pope said these words:

Each nation received the good seed of the apostles'

preaching according to their own mentality and culture. Each local church grew with its own personality, its own customs, its own personal way of celebrating the same mysteries, without harming the unity of faith and the community of all in charity, and the respect for the order established by Christ of which the Holy Spirit has given us a new experience in our time and in the Council. If unity is only Catholic when it fully respects the legitimate diversity of each, diversity is only Catholic in its turn in the measure with which it respects unity, serves charity, and contributes to the building up of the Holy People of God.[7]

At the 1974 Synod the Pope accepted the need to find 'a better expression of faith to correspond to the racial, social and cultural milieux' and he spoke about the apostles presenting the Christian message in a 'diversity of languages'. Languages are not mere codes but an integral part of the cultures and symbol systems of peoples. This the Pope acknowledged in the Jerusalem address, as well as in the Rubaga speech (quoted in Chapter Two). Language presupposes 'the style, the character, the genius and the culture' as well as 'the tongue'.[8] The Pope's anxiety, therefore, seems to centre on a theological diversity that might harm the content of the faith. This content, as the Pope points out, must be faithful to the constant tradition of the Church and it must be Catholic, or universal. He is not asserting that the Church's tradition is a static tradition, nor is he equating the Catholic faith with its western expression.

When all is said and done, neither the Declaration of the African Bishops nor the Pope's Address at the Conclusion of the Synod are very helpful in giving us the shape of a theological unity that is truly Catholic, and we are back at Professor Vanneste's argument. A Catholic theological unity is one which interests us all, is relevant to all and is contributed to by all. This means, in effect, a theology deriving from a continuing dialogue between religions and cultures in their reaction to Jesus Christ and his message. The opening words of the Vatican Council's Declaration on Non-Christian Religions makes this very point, that human groups are united in manifesting a common religious concern. Mankind is one and its solidarity must be expressed by each tradition finding a place in a universal Christian theology. Christianity must be able to answer the needs of the different human cultures.

> In our times, when every day men are being drawn closer together and the ties between various peoples are being multiplied, the Church is giving deeper study to her relationship with Non-Christian religions. In her task of fostering unity and love among men, and even among nations, she gives primary consideration in this document to what human beings have in common and to what promotes fellowship among them.
>
> For all peoples comprise a single community, and have a single origin, since God made the whole race of men dwell over the entire face of the earth.... Men look to the various religions for answers to those profound mysteries of the human condition which, today even as in olden times, deeply stir the human heart: What is a man? What is the meaning and purpose of our life? What is goodness and what is sin? What gives rise to our sorrows and to what intent? Where lies the path to true happiness? What is the truth about death, judgement and retribution beyond the grave? What, finally, is that ultimate and unutterable mystery which engulfs our being, and whence we take our rise, and whither our journey leads us?[8]

Since we do not hold a static view of Christian Theology, we must see it as being called to become progressively more Catholic, as the reality of Jesus Christ is confronted and lived by successive human cultures. The Pope's fear of the Church disintegrating at the centre was shared some years ago by Professor Roland Oliver.[9] He saw this as a real danger in Africa, where expansion had been so rapid. However, Dr McVeigh, writing in 1974, sees the only solution in an incarnational type of theology:

> That danger is still a reality. Much depends on the Church's willingness to assess the present position of God in African Christianity and its ability to reorient its message; so that the God who revealed himself fully in Jesus Christ will be able to speak in a new way to the deepest needs of the African heart.[10]

154

The dangers of theological diversity stem from isolation. All the channels of communication must be kept open. There must be a continual exchange of views and information between Christian theologians in different parts of the world, and a forum for this exchange must be maintained. Above all Western Theologians, who still have a virtual monopoly of the subject, must not imagine they are writing 'Catholic Theology' unless they at least consider the possibility of non-western contributions. The task is to build up a dialogical theology, and this is not simply a kind of religious jig-saw puzzle, with the pieces already cut out in different religions and waiting to be put together. Dialogue, as we have tried to describe it in this book, is a dynamic process, and its fruits are still to be seen. This point is well made by Fr Richard de Smet, S.J., speaking of Indian dialogical theology which is considerably further advanced than African dialogical theology.

> Inter-religious dialogue obviously tends to transform the actual plurality of religions into a pluriform religious universalism. Whether this universalism will be attained and whether it will remain pluriaxial or become mono-axial are questions for the future, but what I would like to make clear is that it is not an alpha but an omega point. That universalism is something to be achieved, to be made through converging efforts, not a hidden reality to be uncovered and manifested.[11]

3 Incarnational Theology and Religious Education

The introduction of elements from African Traditional Religion into the religious education syllabuses in Africa can look very like opportunism, in view of the fact that African governments in the post-Independence era are demanding the teaching of the African religious heritage in schools. To some parents and teachers, suspicious of such developments, it can look like this. The reality, however, is very different. Modern theological thinking demands a dialogue with the Non-Christian religions, and such trends must be reflected in the various levels of religious education. The case is the same as for the study of the Bible. Some idea of the complex processes by which the books of the Old and New Testaments have come down to us must be given to school children at their particular level. If this is not done, they will experience a crisis as adults when they realize that the whole truth was withheld from them as children. The same is true for attitudes towards traditional religion. It would be extremely dangerous to inculcate simplistic, negative attitudes into them, and then leave them to discover as adults that, in reality, the Church's approach has now become more subtle and discerning. Already, in the catechetical syllabuses attempts must be made to echo developments in theology, and though there is a necessary time-lag, this effort is praiseworthy.[12]

Another important reason why the youth should be given an up-to-date account of the Church's thinking with regard to African Traditional Religion is that they themselves are situated at the very flash-point of the existing conflict. Not only do they experience the inner conflict of the ordinary Christian at home, but this is overlaid by a new conflict with the Christianity they profess, the conflict aroused by the exaltation of African culture, and by the spirit of materialism and scepticism which prevails in academic circles. If the student comes from a rural background he may have already experienced the structural revolution which is going on in the rural areas, and which, in the opinion of many sociologists, is more far-reaching and more significant than the urban revolution. He is already participating in the modern mentality with its experience of competition, social mobility, emancipation and personalism. He is perplexed by the differences between the Christianity taught in the class-room and the latent, traditional values to which he himself subscribes and which are lived by his own circle of relatives and friends at home. He may not be in sympathy with the Independent Churches or any of the neo-traditional movements, and may affect to despise them, but he observes them as part of the pluralistic world in which he has to find his way. In this pluralistic situation he may not find the organization of the churches either intelligible or attractive; indeed they may correspond to only one segment of his experience, often the school itself. He finds himself adhering to groups or communities in which Christian values are far from explicit. He reads modern African writers who idealize the religious values of the African past, who lament the passing of traditional cultures, and whose attitude to Christianity is critical, if not frankly hostile. He feels the attraction of political ideology which appeals to African values, and he cannot fail to contrast the reticence of the Church on this subject with the exuberance of the politicians. He runs the risk either of disorientation, or of drift into a sub-human materialism. He needs to be taught how to accept the changing situation and take up a constructive attitude towards it. Above all he needs to learn how to make his profession of Christianity into an integrating force in his own life and in the society to which he belongs.

The work of dialogue is a very important part of the task of the religious educator. Only he can articulate African traditional religious values for the student in logical forms which relate to his needs in a technological society and which interact with a sophisticated understanding of Christianity. Without being disloyal to his own tradition, he must, nevertheless, adopt a self-critical attitude towards it, and his resolve to serve the moral goods and values in African Traditional Religion must be sincere. He must select values which not only parallel Christian ones, but which develop and complement them. He must also show how Christianity can develop and complement African values in their turn, but he must be honest about irreconcilable conflicts.

In the class-room it is obvious that the 'anti-pagan' approach, and anything which savours of it, must be completely ruled out. African Traditional Religion is not to be introduced into the class-room in order to be condemned outright. Such an approach, even if it were tenable, is no longer possible. However, there is an allied approach which some might be tempted to employ. This could be called 'the insufficiency approach'. According to this method, a fairly accurate description of African Traditional Religion is given, but the teacher is concerned, throughout the lesson, to show that Christianity in its present form is superior, and that it completes and develops it at every point. Being certain of one's own identity is not the same thing as feeling superior to others. From many points of view, traditional religion may be insufficient, but that is not to say that Christianity in western form speaks to the real needs of Africans. Bishop Jacobs makes the point well in the introduction to his *Christian Theology in Africa*.

Bantu theology has good sociology producing a good culture, but it also has weaknesses and it is losing ground rapidly. Traditional Western Christian Theology has some weaknesses even for Western needs, and often has not been seen to be relevant to African problems. Now we must come to the Scriptures to discover God's answers to our own problems here in our day. If *my* baby gets sick, I think in scientific terms of the blood, the germs and medicine. If Wambura's baby gets sick, he asks Why? and Who? He begins to look in the community and to the ancestors for the person who has brought on the disease. The Scriptures have the answers for both of us. But now our task is to find the answer for Wambura.[13]

The insufficiency approach is very far from fulfilling the injunction of the Vatican Council's Declaration on Non-Christian Religions 'to acknowledge, preserve and promote' the spiritual goods of these religions.[14]

More acceptable is what may be called 'the seeds of the Gospel approach'. This is very like the insufficiency approach, but instead of stressing a lack, it makes the point that traditional religious values have an inner dynamic which makes them reach out to a further manifestation within Christianity. A good example might be polygamous marriage. Polygamy does not exist as a social institution merely for the satisfaction of male lust. It is there to serve a variety of social needs, the extended family community, the avoidance of childless marriages, caring for widows and so on. The loving relationships engendered by polygamous marriage are good in themselves. However, this manifestation of love in a plurality of unions and households, calls out for a further manifestation of a more exclusive kind of love in a monogamous union. It does not contradict it.

The seeds of the Gospel approach runs the risk of becoming indistinguishable from the insufficiency approach, if Non-Christian values are not credited with any enduring role after the proclamation of Christianity. Non-Christian religions do have a subsequent role to play, either in dialogue with Christianity, or in an original contribution to the development of Christianity itself. The teacher must make it clear that African traditional religion is not simply a preparation for the Gospel as we know it now in the contemporary Church. Rather it paves the way for the Christianity of the future, which hopefully will be more universal. It even paves the way for the era of 'the whole Christ' when God will be all in all. Hence the importance of maintaining a dialogue, rather than indulging in condemnation or expressions of superiority.

The only realistic approach is the dialogical approach— an interchange which takes account of all the factors. It recognizes the truth of the anticipation of Christianity by African traditional religion and of the so-called 'seeds of the Gospel', but it also takes account of those elements of the Christian tradition which do not have an obvious echo in African tradition as well as elements in African tradition which are either indifferent or which could offer new insights. Such elements would be, for example, African formulations which are superior to current Christian formulations or insights that could reawaken or draw out dormant and latent themes in the Christian tradition.

In all of this dialogue, the Christian teacher has to remember to recognize the privileged place of Scripture. It is true in a sense, as it is sometimes said, that African Traditional Religion is Africa's Old Testament, but it can only be understood as such by reference to the Jewish Old Testament. It can only derive its value as a preparation for the Christian Gospel when it is compared to, and understood in the light of, the preparation for Christ as a historical person in the history of the Jewish people.

Enough has already been said to underline the importance of the discipline of social anthropology to the religious educator. Its importance lies, not only in providing a correct understanding of African traditional religious ideas, but also in placing these ideas in their total life context. It also demands respect for the characteristic African forms of communication, symbolism and ritual, and provides the methodology for their analysis. It is often asked whether all of African religious tradition is useful to the religious teacher. While recognizing a hierarchy of values within African tradition, I would answer 'yes'. On the analogy of Scripture, I would say in St Paul's words to Timothy: all of African tradition 'can profitably be used for teaching, for refuting error, for guiding people's lives and teaching them to be holy'. (2 Tm. 3: 16-17.) In other words, using a value from

African tradition does not mean that it has to be approved. Ideas and practices can be selected for praise or blame. Moreover, the ideas and practices selected do not always have to come from the students' own experience. Many values which are disappearing can be used as examples and will find a ready response in the minds of African students who are prepared to appeal to the past in their search for a present identity. On the other hand one has to avoid anti-quarianism at all costs. There is a real danger in looking at African Traditional Religion as if it were a past phenomenon and of simply contrasting it with present life. Search must be made for continuity and synthesis. To sum up, the method for introducing African Traditional Religion into the religion syllabus should be a selective and applied method. It should select whatever is relevant to the adult community in the modern situation and to the student as a future member of that community. It should then be rigorously applied, so that the student can discover and express a meaning and a purpose in his life on African terms.

4 Conclusion

We began the enquiry which constitutes this book with a look at the bridges and barriers which, in general, facilitate or impede a meeting between Christianity and the African Religions. From there we looked at some of the expectations of an African Christian Theology and came to the conclusion that it has to be a dialogical theology. It has to take into account the religious traditions of Non-Christian Africa. There then arose the problem central to the whole discussion: How are we to study African Traditional Religion? The answer was a complex one and the examples we have provided show the kind of *minutiae* into which we must descend. Broadly speaking, the study must be scientific and systematic. It was then that we asked the even more fundamental question: Can there be a real communication between cultures, and particularly between a science that is an off-shoot of western culture and a non-western culture? Perhaps surprisingly, the affirmative answer provided a pointer to the theological universalism which is the goal of the dialogical process. The conditions of a fast changing, pluralistic society also demand this type of theologizing. In this final chapter, we have seen how there is a growing realization in the Roman

Catholic Church of the need for a ministry of dialogue with the Non-Christian Religions and of an Incarnational Theology. Finally, we drew some practical conclusions for the religious educator. At certain points, during the discussion, the process of dialogue was at work, but inevitably the book as a whole was a discussion about dialogue, rather than an entry into dialogue. It is to be hoped that, as a methodological enquiry, it has helped to clear the air a little further for the urgent task of writing African Christian Theology.

Notes

1. E.g. *Developing in Christ and Christian Living Today*, syllabuses for African Secondary Schools, Forms I-IV, published by Geoffrey Chapman.

2. Sastre, R., 1957, 'Liturgie Romaine et Négritude', in *Des Prètres Noirs s'Interrogent*, Paris, p. 163.

3. Vanneste, A., 1968, 'Théologie Universelle et Théologie Africaine', in *Renouveau de l'Eglise et Nouvelles Eglises*, Kinshasa, p. 173.

4. 'Synod Bishops from Africa Issue Declaration', *AMECEA Documentation Service*, no. 11/74/2, pp. 2-3.

5. 'Holy Father's Address at Conclusion of Synod of Bishops, 26th October, 1974', *l'Osservatore Romano*, N.45 (345), November 7th, 1974, p. 9.

6. *Ibid.*

7. Address of Pope Paul VI to the Oriental Rite Bishops, in St Anne's Church, Jerusalem, January 1964, Bulletin of the White Fathers, *Petit Echo*, 2, 1964.

8. *Nostra Aetate*, 1.

9. Oliver, R., 1952, *The Missionary Factor in East Africa*, London, p. 291.

10. McVeigh, M. J., 1974, *God in Africa*, Cape Cod, Massachusetts, p. 182.

11. de Smet, R., S.J., 1974, 'Suggestions for an Indian Dialogical Theology', in *Outlook*, Vol. XIV, no. 4, p. 122.

12. Cf. note 1, above.

13. Jacobs, D. R., 1966, *Christian Theology in Africa*, (mimeographed), Mount Joy, Pennsylvania, p. 1.

Index

Issanzu tribe (Tanzania), 62-63

Jacobs, Bishop Donald, 157
Jerusalem, 152
Jesus Christ, 30-31, 113-114, 153-154, 159
Jews, 113-114, 159
John, St, the Evangelist, 121
Judgement, 58, 121-122
Juju, 106

Kagamé, Rev. Fr Alexis, 24-25
Kalenjin Tribe (Kenya), 63
Kampala City (Uganda), 6, 20-21, 23, 145
Kaunda, President Kenneth, of Zambia, 35
Kenya, 62, 64, 99, 119
Kenya, Mount, 116
Kiga Tribe (Uganda), 63-64
Kikuyu Tribe (Kenya), 99-100, 117, 123-124
Kilanga I, Chief of the Bungu, 90-91
Kimbu Tribe (Tanzania), 38, 61-68, 70, 74, 76-77, 89-93, 102-103, 125
Kintu, King of Buganda, 50, 116, 148
Kimambo, Prof. I. N., 48, 50
Kinshasa City (Zaïre), 149
Koenig, Cardinal Franz, 38
Komba, Bishop James, 11
Konongo Tribe (Tanzania), 125
Kopytoff, I., 124, 126
Kuhn, Thomas, 135
Kuria Tribe (Kenya and Tanzania), 62-63

Lake Rukwa, 61, 74, 89-90, 93
Lake Victoria Nyanza, 116
Leopard-skin priests, 83-84, 86, 88
Lévi-Strauss, Prof. Claude, 27, 112
Lévy-Bruhl, Lucien, 25, 133
Liberation Theology, 29
Lienhardt, Dr R. G., 79, 84-85, 87, 101, 111, 117
Life-crisis rituals, 123-124

Life-themes, 112
Lightning, 81-82, 92
Liminality, 35
Limited comparative approach, 51-53, 79-94
Limuru Conference on the Historical Study of African Religion, 3, 61, 77
Logic, 138
Lovanium University (Kinshasa), 149
Luguru Tribe (Tanzania), 104
Luo, Central, Tribe (Uganda), 107-108
Luo Tribe (Kenya), 115-116
Luyia Tribe (Kenya), 109

Makerere University (Uganda), 3-4, 107
Malawi, 103, 148
Manchester University, 51
Marakwet Tribe (Kenya), 63
Masters of the Fishing Spear, 86-88
Mbiti, Rev. Prof. John S., 11, 23, 46, 48-49, 50
M'bona cult of the Zambezi Valley, 51
Mboya, Tom, 35
Mbugwe Tribe (Tanzania), 62-63
McLennan, J. F., 52
McVeigh, Dr Malcolm, 154
Mediators, 58, 102-105, 122, 125, 126
Memorial, 58, 113-117
Mende Tribe (Sierra Leone), 57, 104-105
Meru Tribe (Kenya), 62-63, 99, 116, 119
Methodists, 16
Mukasa, Ganda divinity, 50
Multi-dimensional approaches, 58-59
Murdock, Prof. G. P., 41, 52
Murphree, Prof. Marshall W., 15
Muslims, 2, 90
Mwachiluwi, Chief of Ubungu, 90, 93

Nairobi, University of (Kenya), 50

Namibia (South West Africa), 122

Near East, 145

Neckebrouck, Rev. Fr V., 28, 34

Negritude, 22, 29, 47

Neill, Bishop Stephen, 38

Ngoni Tribe (Tanzania), 90

Nieboer, H. J., 52

Niger Basin, 47

Non-Christians, 18, 38, 145, 148, 154

Nuer Tribe (Sudan), 79-89, 101, 103, 123

Nupe Tribe (Nigeria), 106

Nyakyusa Tribe (Tanzania), 10, 127

Nyamwezi Tribe (Tanzania), 62-66, 74, 76-77, 90-91, 96

Nyamiti, Rev. Fr Charles, 11

Nyerere, President Julius K., of Tanzania, 35

Nyikang, Shilluk divinity (Sudan), 50

Nyisamba section of the Kimbu Tribe (Tanzania), 62, 66, 68, 74

Nyitumba section of the Kimbu Tribe (Tanzania), 50, 62, 66, 67, 69, 74, 76, 90, 91

Nyoro Tribe (Uganda), 63-64, 117

Nyungu-ya-Mawe, Chief of Kiwele, 91

Ogot, Prof. B. A., 50, 116

Okot p'Bitek, Dr, 25-26, 107-108, 131

Old Testament, Africa's, 159

Oliver, Prof. Roland, 154

Pare Tribe (Tanzania), 50, 62-63

Parrinder, Rev. Prof. Geoffrey, 43-44, 48, 50

Particularist approach, 12, 38-42

Paul VI, Pope, 20-21, 35, 113, 121-122, 151-152, 153-154

Paul, St, 121

Pender-Cudlip, Patrick, 70

Pentecostalism, 13

Philosophy, 10, 23-27

Pimbwe Tribe (Tanzania), 62-63, 76

Pluralism, 3, 20, 30, 32, 136, 139-143, 151-152, 160

Popper, Karl, 8-9

Post-Christians, 8

Prayer, 14, 58, 95, 117, 127

Praeparatio Evangelica (Preparation for the Gospel), 16-17, 23

Preaching, 29-30

Priesthood, 12

Protestants, 23

Proverbs, 25

Pygmies, 98-99, 101

Radcliffe-Brown, A. R., 52

Rain-making, 50, 69, 75, 91, 93

Ranger, Prof. T. O., 48

Reincarnation, 57

Religious Education, 155-161

Rhodesia, 15, 127

Ritual, 7, 12, 20, 26, 28, 50, 55, 69, 70, 93, 87, 97, 112-113, 123-124, 127

Roman Catholics, 1, 16, 20, 23, 145-146

Rubaga Cathedral, Kampala (Uganda), 20, 153

Rukwa Plain, 66, 89-90, 92

Rwanda, 119-120

Sacrament, 114

Sacrifice, 82-84, 86-87, 88, 117

Salvation Theology, 9

Sawyerr, Rev. Canon Harry, 11, 56-57, 112

Sastre, Bishop Robert, 21, 149

Schapera, Prof. I., 52-53

Schoffeleers, Rev. Dr M., 51

Schonenberger, Rev. Fr P., 65

Science, 3, 26, 34, 118, 132, 134-139

Scripture, 13, 30-31, 63, 113-115, 127, 143, 156, 158-159

Secular Theology, 34

Secularism, 56, 119

'Seeds of the Gospel' approach, 16, 17, 158